Praise for Deborah Taylor[
Freezer Cooking Met

Taylor-Hough, Deborah.

Frozen assets lite and
easy

"*Frozen Assets* will prove to be the hands-down authority on once-a-month cooking."—Susan R. Sands, publisher, *Home Words* magazine

"This book offers relief to those tired of eating restaurant fare or expensive, over-packaged c[ ]mended."
—*Library Journa*

"Contains recipe[ ]um value from your food[ ] are into efficiency and w[ ]s a must-have."—Amazon

DATE DUE

"Finally, a realis[ ]m scratch with the conven[ ]ublisher, *Cheapskate Mon*

"This cookbook[ ]while still providing a nutr[ ]

"This book belc[ ]d money-savers a busy far[ ]r

"Finally, a bc[ ] steps."
—Sherry Sta[

"Whether you[ ] benefit from this book

"*Frozen Assets*[ ]a Stuck, advice colum[

"And she's done an impressive job with this book, which outlines step-by-step the shopping, cooking and freezing processes that have worked so well."
—Copley News Service

"Details a plan for cooking and freezing in quantity, with grocery lists, shopping lists, storage tips and dollar-stretching hints. The recipes are simple and straightforward, using everyday ingredients."—*Atlanta Journal*

"A perfect gift for a busy homemaker."—The *News-Herald* newspapers

"Provides shopping lists and delicious recipes that will help you save time in the kitchen and money in the grocery store."—*The Oak Ridger*, Tennessee

"Taylor-Hough's recipes are easy, with a minimum amount of ingredients and labor. And she presents the plan with an eye toward flexibility, allowing cooks to adapt the freeze-ahead plan to their own palates and checkbooks."—*Johnson City Press*

"Offers kid-tested recipes that are easy and affordable."—*The Oregonian*

"Cooks looking to save time without resorting to expensive convenience food will find this book helpful."—*Herald-Journal*

"[This] book outlines a step-by-step plan to one dedicated day in the kitchen that will provide breakfasts, lunches and dinners for the following month."—*Detroit News*

"A cookbook well worth a second look."—*The Pilot*, North Carolina

"Just about everyone will find the planning and organizational tips valuable."
—*The Light Connection*

"The book is a one-stop resource for those looking to increase their time at the family table and decrease time spent in the kitchen and drive-through lanes."
—*The Cookbook Collectors' Exchange*

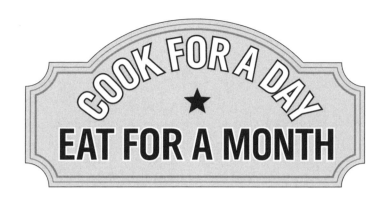

FROZEN ASSETS

LITE AND EASY

COOK FOR A DAY

★

EAT FOR A MONTH

FROZEN ASSETS

LITE AND EASY

DEBORAH TAYLOR-HOUGH

SOURCEBOOKS, INC.®
NAPERVILLE, ILLINOIS

Sourcebooks and the colophon are registered trademarks of Sourcebooks, Inc.

Published by Sourcebooks, Inc.
P.O. Box 4410, Naperville, Illinois 60567-4410
(630) 961-3900
Fax: (630) 961-2168
www.sourcebooks.com

Originally published in 2002 by Champion Press, Ltd.

Library of Congress Cataloging-in-Publication Data

Taylor-Hough, Deborah.
 Frozen assets lite and easy : cook for a day, eat for a month / by Deborah Taylor-Hough.
  p. cm.
 1. Cookery (Frozen foods) 2. Quick and easy cookery. 3. Low-fat diet—Recipes. 4. Low-calorie diet—Recipes. I. Title.
 TX828.T39 2009
 641.6'153—dc22
                          2009002569

Printed and bound in the United States of America.
VP 10 9 8 7 6 5 4 3 2

Also by Deborah Taylor-Hough

Frozen Assets

Dedication

This book is dedicated to my mother-in-law, Jean Hough, whose kitchen organizational skills, fabulous parties, and gifts of hospitality are truly awe-inspiring. Thank you for your example!

CONTENTS

ACKNOWLEDGMENTS

I just want to thank everyone who offered moral support or had input into this book during its production and writing: Brook Noel, Leanne Ely, Q, Catherine Levison, Lisa Morales, Miriam Roush, Karen Jogerst, Teri Brown, Larry Wilson, Gary Foreman, Gina Dalquest, Chris Saunders, *Simple Times* readers, participants from my frugal-living message board, the Frozen Assets email list members, Stuart, Kelsey, Ian, Shannon, and Dad.

1
★ ★ ★

FROZEN ASSETS

Those of you familiar with my first book may be wondering, "Why another *Frozen Assets* book?"

Good question. The original *Frozen Assets: How To Cook For a Day and Eat For a Month* was written specifically to help readers learn realistic and inexpensive ways to apply bulk-cooking methods to their regular family-meal planning. The emphasis in the first *Frozen Assets* was on two commodities in high demand: time and money. For many, making the switch to eating home-cooked meals every night rather than a regular diet of fast food and pizza delivery also created a healthier lifestyle. However, over the years, readers have contacted me looking for simple meal plans with lower-fat recipes. I've also heard from readers looking for vegetarian fare to add to their freezer-meal recipe collections.

The recipes in *Frozen Assets Lite and Easy* are an answer for those of you looking to apply the same time-saving and easy cooking methods to lower-calorie meals. While you can still expect to cut your budget significantly by using these bulk preparation methods, the lower-fat recipes tend to use more expensive ingredients than the original recipes of the first *Frozen Assets* book. Using the recipes and meal plans in that book, I was able to shave $400 off our family food budget during a time when saving money was a top priority in my life. This added up to $24,000 over a five-year period!

Yet the principles of *Frozen Assets Lite and Easy* cooking will still allow you to trim your food budget, as well as your fat. Buying in bulk and using all the foods before they perish will greatly reduce trips to the store, and avoid the chance of impulse purchasing and throwing away yet another vegetable gone bad. It will also allow you to take advantage of store sales and specials, as you'll see when we explore the mini-session methods.

Healthy Transitions

The reasons people choose to start eating healthier are varied. Some of us want or need to shed a few extra pounds. Some are interested in a generally healthier lifestyle. Some have more philosophical reasons for avoiding meat or other food items. Others face health-related dietary restrictions.

In the food department of life, I've definitely been my own worst enemy over the years. Eating healthy has long been appealing to me…but not so easily attainable. I can still remember the first time I browsed through my well-loved copy of *Laurel's Kitchen* and dreamed of all the whole foods my family would soon be eating. And eat healthy, we did! For a while…

I remember baking my own breads, tenderly kneading each loaf by hand in my favorite oversized mixing bowl. This was in the good old days, before automatic bread machines. I relished the entire process of baking fresh, homemade bread—the taste, the feel, the smell. For a while…

I remember happily replacing meat in our regular family recipes with tofu and texturized vegetable protein (TVP). What a great feeling to feed my family lower-fat, healthier foods. With a tremendous sense of accomplishment, I prepared our new healthier meals. For a while…

Are you beginning to sense a pattern here? It seemed my best intentions were constantly being waylaid by life. Whether it was a financial setback, a premature baby, an extended time of bedrest during a difficult pregnancy, or an overly busy schedule, something always pushed me back into the realm of what was normal and comfortable in the food department of my life. The old expression, "Life's what happens when you make other plans," was certainly holding true in my eating and cooking regimens. I continually found myself coasting back down to lower levels of eating. I was on a never-ending roller coaster ride. And I wanted off.

I knew I'd hit rock bottom when I was starting to plan our family meals around the local fast-food restaurant's choice of children's meal toys. Have you ever known anyone on a first-name basis with the pizza delivery guy, with the kids calling out when the doorbell rang, "Mommy, Bob's here with the pizza!"? The regular lady at the local drive-thru would comment about how she hadn't seen us for a while if we didn't come to her window for a week or so.

Things were bad. Really bad.

But I knew I needed more than just an outward change in my eating habits. I needed to find some sort of inner motivation that would keep me on the right path, no matter what distractions and detours life sent my way.

The biggest obstacle that kept me from pursuing healthy eating habits was my personal time constraints. Like many people today, I didn't have time to get home-cooked meals on the table regularly, much less to take the time to actually prepare something nutritious and healthy.

Then something happened that completely changed my wishy-washy approach to healthful eating.

One morning, I was showering and discovered what every woman dreads: a lump. A sizeable lump. Suddenly I was at the doctor's office having X-rays and ultrasounds, and before I really had time to fathom the full repercussions of this new chapter in my life, I was being scheduled for a surgical lumpectomy and biopsy. The earliest they could schedule the procedure was several weeks away, so I found myself in a waiting mode, trying not to obsess about my health, but finding myself helplessly evaluating everything in my life.

It seemed that in one swift, life-changing moment I'd gone from peacefully going about my quiet little life to suddenly examining every moment and activity in light of the question, "What if…?" What if I have cancer? What if I get horribly sick? What if I die? What if I don't live to see my children grow up? What if this is my last summer here on Earth? What if…

My entire life was now under a high-power microscope. I'd find myself looking at an activity and thinking, "Is this how I would want to spend my time if this were the last week of my life?" More often than not, the answer was a resounding, "No!" Suddenly everything stood out like a relief map. It was easy to identify priorities in a way I never had before. I had lived for a long time with a clear set of priorities before me, but my priorities took on new meaning as I sensed a new urgency.

My children. My husband. My faith. My church. These priorities suddenly grew in importance as my focus changed. Other activities, like writing, public speaking, Internet activities, and even mundane things like housework, lessened their hold over my life. It wasn't that those things ceased to be important, but their placement in the way I chose to spend my time and energy changed.

I even found myself looking at where I lived and deciding that if I were facing the end of my time, one of my biggest regrets was living at the end of a cul-de-sac in a standard housing development. My heart had always been in the country, with horses and acreage. If my life were over, I found that I truly regretted not having done what was necessary to make that dream come true somehow. Raising my children in suburbia wasn't what I'd wanted for my life. I found myself wondering when I'd started living someone else's dreams.

But probably the biggest refocusing that occurred was in the area of my physical health. For many years, I'd been eating a poor diet and living a sedentary lifestyle. And my poor body showed it: out of shape, overweight, and out of breath.

Suddenly, I confronted my physical health in a new way and decided I needed to make some changes…now! In addition to regular aerobic exercise and strength training, I also decided to change my eating habits. Nothing drastic—I didn't set out to lose forty pounds in two weeks, or anything like that. But by eating lower-fat, healthier meals and being careful about not overdoing it on sweets or second helpings, I hoped to change my health in simple—yet profound—ways. After starting this lower-fat, more-balanced approach to eating, I lost ten pounds in the first week…and I wasn't doing anything drastic at all. My goal hadn't necessarily been weight loss. I'm much more concerned with maintaining a healthier lifestyle in general. But as my body reacts to the new ways of eating and exercising, I'm sure the weight will come off too. But in the meantime, I'm feeling better and stronger than I have in a long, long time.

This book contains many of the recipes I've been preparing for myself and my family lately. Hopefully, the meal plans will help you and your family in your pursuit of healthy, vital lives.

SAVING TIME, SAVING MONEY

What if I told you I had a way for you to gain an extra hour each day… or seven hours per week … or nearly thirty hours per month? Would you start wondering if I'd fallen out of the crib onto my head a few too many times as a baby? Well, this deal is for real. I have a commodity to offer that's more valuable than gold … or land … or diamonds. That precious gem I can offer you is called: Time!

Wouldn't you love to free up quantities of time each and every day? Time that could be spent sitting down with your spouse on the couch, actually putting your feet up after work for a few undisturbed moments? Wouldn't your children relish curling up in a parent's lap for a cuddle and a chapter from the family's latest read-aloud book before dinner?

And wouldn't you really love having an easy answer to that perennial question, "What's for dinner?"

What's for dinner tonight could be as simple as something you whip together in fifteen to twenty minutes: Salisbury steak, homemade fish chowder, Aunt Emily's favorite lasagna, roast turkey with all the fixings, marinated chicken breasts, or whatever else your family enjoys eating. And you won't spend an hour or two slaving over a hot stove every night to achieve this culinary miracle. It might just require the minor effort of throwing a baking dish into the oven and forgetting it for an hour. Or stirring something over a stovetop burner just until it's heated through. Make a salad, slice some French bread fresh from the corner bakery, and voila, you'll have a dinner that would make Martha Stewart proud!

Crisis Meal Planning

If your home is anything like mine, you've probably found that five o'clock each evening is one of the most hectic times of the day. Mom and Dad are just finishing up a long day of work at home or at the office. The kids are hungry and tired after a full day of school and afternoon sports. It's time to fix supper—or at least we should be getting dinner started if we want to eat a meal before midnight! But what's for dinner tonight? Well, your guess is probably as good as mine...and it seems like more often than not, nobody knows! So the whole family hops in the car and heads through the local drive-thru for the third time in a week.

Someone I know once called this "crisis" meal planning. Each night's dinner is the latest in a string of mealtime crisis management decisions. Everyone's tired. The kids are hungry. The whining is starting in earnest. What's a parent to do?

"What will we have to eat? Um...well...I just heard that Fred's Diner is having a sale on cheeseburgers this week. Let's go! Everyone in the car!"

Rather than planning ahead to prevent panic and poor nutritional choices, many families coast through their days without giving a thought to dinner—only to discover they've crashed headlong into that nightly mealtime crisis once again.

Cooking ahead for the freezer can be the answer to this all-too-frequent mealtime dilemma. The process of cooking an entire month's worth of meals in one day is an efficient and cost-saving alternative for many families, but spending eight hours in the kitchen may be daunting for some who would like to try this method. The mini session is the perfect answer for these people.

Whether you choose to triple recipes during your regular meal preparations, cook a full month of meals at a time, or simply choose a mini session or two, you'll find this method will save not only your time, but also your money and your sanity. There will be no more crisis meal planning; you'll have dinner on the table regularly with little more fuss than heating a thawed freezer meal and adding a quick salad or side dish.

The Art of the Mini Session

I've discovered as people become more adept and experienced at cooking for the freezer, they often switch from doing a full one-day-each-month cooking frenzy to a simpler process, which I call mini sessions. A mini session consists of choosing one main ingredient, such as chicken, and then preparing a group of chicken recipes in a single afternoon or evening. A mini session usually involves only an hour or two of cooking, rather than the eight to ten hours often required for a complete month of cooking.

By waiting for main ingredients to go on sale at your local market, you can stock up on large quantities and take advantage of great prices. For example, if you stock up on lean ground beef at this week's sale, a relatively short mini session could easily supply you with five to ten ground-beef meals tucked away in the freezer. When chicken goes on sale later in the month, you can add another five to ten meals to your personal stash of Frozen Assets. By simply purchasing and cooking in bulk as you follow the sale flyers from the grocery store, you can save a great deal of time and money without ever investing an entire day in a monthly cooking session.

This new book, *Frozen Assets Lite and Easy,* focuses on the mini session method, but that doesn't mean it isn't flexible and easily adapted for those readers who prefer the one-day-a-month procedure. If you want to do a full month of cooking in one day, simply double or triple several mini sessions and prepare them together in one day. A full day of cooking for the freezer is essentially just a series of mini sessions. Most cooks will first prepare all their ground meat recipes, then the chicken recipes, then the spaghetti sauce-based recipes, and then vegetarian or bean recipes.

The great thing about breaking this all down into mini sessions is that it allows you to build a month's worth of recipes around your family's specific tastes. Instead of trying to pull apart a Thirty-Day Meal Plan and change one unpopular recipe, you can build your menus around mini sessions that the family enjoys. Many people also find it easier to build their own mini sessions to incorporate into their Frozen Assets regimen. Be flexible. Take your favorite recipes from *Frozen Assets*, and build them into a mini session. Build your own mini sessions. Use the mini sessions offered in this book. Combine all three ideas. Whichever you choose, a boundless array of easy meal choices await you!

But Isn't It a Leftover?

Many people worry that eating meals from the freezer will be like having leftovers every night. But it's not. You won't be eating something that's been cooked completely, reheated, and then reheated again. You're eating food that's either been frozen before cooking, so it's cooked up fresh on serving day, or you're eating food that's been cooked just until barely done, frozen, and then reheated just enough to serve. If food is cooked and stored properly, frozen dinners can be as tasty as fresh.

3

★ ★ ★

EASIER COOKING
FOR EASIER LIVING

I first started cooking ahead for the time-saving benefits. It helped bring our family together again around the table. But I was quickly surprised by another benefit that I didn't foresee. Our grocery bill went down by almost $400 per month! I couldn't believe it! Some of the money we saved was because we had been eating out quite frequently, quickly running down to the corner for inexpensive tacos because I didn't have time to cook dinner. Now we always have time for dinner at home. We eat out when we want to, not because we feel we have to. Going out to eat has become a special treat rather than an expensive and unhealthy way of life.

By cooking ahead, I was able to begin buying commonly used items in bulk. I was also planning my menus ahead of time. Just the planning ahead and bulk buying saves a lot of money. But $400 per month? Wow! And that was the average I was shaving off our grocery bill each month. Sometimes we saved even more than that. This method also eliminates waste, and because I don't go to the store nearly as often as I used to, it also cuts down on those expensive impulse buys at the market.

I can take full advantage of sales at the grocery store, planning menus around the weekly specials. If ground beef is on sale, I'll buy a large amount and then prepare a quantity of ground-beef recipes and put them in the freezer. Rather than doing a full month of cooking, I'll do what I refer to as a Ground Beef Mini Session. This involves preparing a week or two of ground beef recipes to intersperse with the chicken or tofu recipes I prepared during an earlier chicken or tofu mini session.

With a combination of these mini sessions, I can stash away Frozen Assets for the next two or three months. But in addition to the time- and money-saving benefits, I discovered many other perks.

Hospitality

Frozen meals can be used for hospitality and outreach. Dinner parties are a breeze. If we want to spontaneously invite people over after church, it's not a difficult ordeal. I know I have things in the freezer that I can quickly and easily heat and serve. You can have meals available for the sick, or for people in need. Bringing a couple of frozen meals to a new mother or a grieving family can bring a touch of sanity to an otherwise stressful time of life. I don't even have to think about it or plan for it. I just grab something from the freezer and go.

Financial Freedom

Not only did cooking ahead solve the meal-planning and time issues, it also provided me with a way to help our family's financial situation. Money was quite tight, and I had been thinking of getting a part-time job to help make ends meet. I found cutting back a bit on what I was spending on groceries could mean the difference between remaining at home with my children or going back to work. I wouldn't cut back on the amount of food we ate, so we still ate well, but by being conscientious about meal planning and buying on sale, we shaved sizeable amounts off our monthly food budget. Saving $400 per month from our approximately $700 per month grocery budget became my part-time job. Over the course of five years, I spent $24,000 less on groceries!

No More Kitchen Slavery

During those rare times when I run out of my Frozen Assets stash, it's a rude awakening to see just how difficult daily food preparation is in a busy home. As I often say when doing my workshops, I like cooking—I just don't like it every day! Considering all the planning and actual preparation time for each meal, the kitchen can seem to be a harsh taskmaster, not even allowing time off for good behavior. The dailyness of cooking wears us down quickly. By having meals ready to go in the freezer, I find that the joy of cooking has been restored for me. When I do decide to cook a special meal, it's a joy, and not just another chore to be accomplished as quickly as possible. I also have more time and energy for fun cooking, such as baking cookies with my children or making fresh, hot gingerbread on a cold winter evening.

Restoring the Family Dinner Hour

Recently, there was a story in my local newspaper about the disappearance of the family dinner hour. With more and more double-income families and children involved in numerous after-school and sports activities, the family dinner hour has gone the way of the dinosaur.

Yet my family sits down together for dinner at least five times each week. How often do you sit down as a family at the table for a leisurely meal? Four times a week? Twice? Once? I'm not a superwoman. I'm simply someone who discovered a way to reap the benefits of advanced planning and preparation. Now, these benefits can be yours. I'll show you how to make it happen, step-by-step. If you'd like to restore this time-honored tradition in your home, cooking for the freezer can be the solution. So what are you waiting for? Let's get started.

4
★ ★ ★

COOKING FOR THE FREEZER 101

I recommend that people start this process gradually. If the idea of a full month of cooking sounds overwhelming, start small. If two weeks sounds more doable, try cooking ahead for two weeks. Or one week.

But if cooking for even a week at a time sounds like more than you can tackle, try this: in the course of your normal cooking, triple your recipes. If you're preparing lasagna, make three—one for eating tonight and two for the freezer. Tomorrow night, do the same thing with a different recipe. After one week of tripling your regular meals and freezing two prepared recipes of each meal, you'll have two additional weeks of meals with almost no extra effort. It's really not much harder to prepare three lasagnas than it is to prepare one, or to make a large pot of spaghetti sauce rather than a single family-size serving and freeze the extra amount in meal-size servings.

If you think cooking ahead is a process you'd like to try, but you're unsure of the amount of work involved, ease into it. Start out doubling and tripling recipes as you go through your week. Maybe do a ground beef mini session the next time there's a sale at the grocery store. What you will find is that you will start saving time and money, and you won't be doing this in an overwhelming or difficult manner. Each time you pull one of those meals out of the freezer, you'll be pleased.

Small-Freezer Syndrome

Many people tell me they only have a small fridge-top freezer, so they don't think they can do a full month of meals. That was my excuse for not trying this method at first, but I've found that with practice, I can pack a full thirty meals in my refrigerator freezer. The last time I did a big cooking day, I counted forty-four meals in my small freezer. I have a separate freezer now, but I usually use it for stocking things like ice cream or bread I find on sale at the bakery thrift store. I keep my prepared meals in the small kitchen freezer, where they're easily accessible.

Probably the most practical suggestion for people with a small freezer is to use zip-top freezer bags. The bags take up a lot less room than bulkier storage containers, such as plastic boxes or aluminum pans. If you freeze your freezer bags flat, you can stand them on end after they're frozen solid. Your freezer shelf will look like it contains record albums filled with frozen food, and you won't experience a landslide of frozen packages when you open the freezer door.

Clear out all nonessentials on cooking day if you only have a small freezer. When I only had the small freezer, I would wait until midmonth to stock up on things like ice cream or frozen bread. I used this cooking technique for over three years with only a small freezer, so it can be done. It just takes careful planning and packing.

To save space, you can also prepare sauces to serve over pasta or rice, but don't make the pasta or rice ahead of time. Instead, cook the pasta or rice at serving time. Usually, the sauce is the time-consuming part of fixing dinner, so by fixing the pasta or rice fresh, you'll have a better-tasting meal and you'll be able to use your freezer space more efficiently.

Freezer Containers

I want to assure you that you don't need to hold a party and buy expensive plastic boxes. Any food-grade plastic will work. The inexpensive plastic boxes at the grocery store function just fine, but make sure you have storage items with tight-fitting, air-tight lids. If you want to invest money in the higher-quality plastic boxes, by all means feel free to do so. You definitely get what you pay for, and the fancy, expensive home-party boxes usually last for many years and come with replacement guarantees. I just want to assure people that you don't *have* to stock your freezer shelves with designer containers. The only plastic freezer containers I own are the inexpensive ones from the grocery store, and they have served me well for many years.

You can freeze food items in clean, plastic margarine containers if that's all you have, but the seal isn't really air-tight. Therefore, don't freeze these items for longer than two weeks, or the quality of the food will suffer. It's important to remember that margarine containers are safe to freeze food in (they are made of food-grade plastic), but don't reheat your meal in them. They're not microwaveable, and they can seep harmful chemicals into your family's food. Be sure that a plastic container is labeled "microwave safe" before using it to reheat food.

If you have a choice between round and rectangular freezer containers, choose rectangular. These use space more efficiently and take up less room in the freezer.

You can also use disposable aluminum foil pans purchased at the grocery store. These can often be reused several times before needing to be recycled or discarded. Disposable pans are ideal if you're making meals to use to give to others; the recipient won't need to worry about returning your pan or casserole dish. If cleanup is a concern, these pans can be easily thrown away, making cleanup painless.

I've built up a good supply of freezer containers by stocking up on bakeware and other freezeable containers at garage sales and thrift stores. Glass bakeware works fine. When wrapping pans for the freezer, be sure to use good quality heavy-duty freezer foil.

I personally use zip-top freezer bags for most of my food storage needs. Not only do they take up less space than boxes, but the bags are also inexpensive and easy to use. It's important to buy top-quality freezer bags—this isn't the place to cut back, money-wise. There's nothing worse for a freezer-meal cook than to have your entire batch of frozen meals ruined by poor wrapping or broken freezer bags. I recommend double-bagging anything that has a soupy consistency, so you don't end up with a watery mess at the bottom of your refrigerator after the meal thaws. Sometimes bags can develop small holes, or the zip-top can open slightly.

You can also make your own freezer pans by lining a casserole dish with foil. Put the food in on top of the foil, freeze the meal until it's solid, and then remove the foil and food from the pan. Finish wrapping the meal, and put it back in the freezer. When it's time to serve the meal, simply place the foil-wrapped meal back into the original pan that was used to mold the frozen meal. Thaw and reheat in the original pan. This method keeps your pans available for other uses during the month.

Labeling Your Freezer Meals

Make sure you label everything carefully and accurately. When food is frozen, many meals look the same. One tomato-based meal will look like a dozen other tomato-based meals. You don't want to play "Guess the Freezer Meal" when you're trying to get your family's dinner on the table each night.

I recommend using Sharpie™ brand permanent markers for labeling. You can actually write directly on the freezer bags and even on the aluminum foil wrappings. I want to emphasize: Don't use any other brand of permanent marker to write on your freezer bags or foil. There are other brands of permanent markers, but Sharpie is the only one I've found that won't wipe off. When I worked in a medical lab, we were required to carry a Sharpie with us at all times. The lab managers wouldn't let us use any other brand of marker. We wrote on beakers, test tubes, Petri dishes, and slides, and then those items went through assorted chemical baths. The labels written with Sharpies wouldn't come off. You don't want to lose your labels, so it's important to use the best labeler available.

Another way of labeling items is to double-bag the food and slip a 3 × 5-inch file card with the name and heating instructions between the freezer bags. The outer bag and the label can both be reused indefinitely with this method, which is especially handy if you prepare the same meals often. You can prepare half a dozen labels ahead of time and not have to spend that time and effort with each cooking session. This way, you can prep the meal quickly and easily without having to dig through a recipe box or cookbook.

What to Freeze, What Not to Freeze

When I started cooking for the freezer, I was amazed to find that more things freeze well than don't. I thought there must be some special criteria for deciphering whether or not a meal would freeze, but almost anything can be frozen. Take a walk down your grocery store's frozen-food aisle sometime and note the wide variety of items that can be frozen ahead.

Foods that Freeze Well

Baked goods (most)

Beans, cooked

Breakfast burritos

Breakfast casseroles

Brownies

Cakes

Calzones

Casseroles

Cookies

Egg rolls

Enchiladas

French toast

Fruit sauces

Fudge

Grains, cooked, such as rice, barley, and bulgur

Hamburger patties, uncooked

Quiche

Quick breads

Lasagna

Main dishes

Manicotti

Marinated meats

Mashed potatoes

Meatballs

Meatloaf

Meat pies

Muffins

Pancakes

Pies

Pot pies

Poultry

Roasted meats, such as beef, chicken, lamb, and pork

Sandwiches

Sauces

Sloppy joes

Soups

Stuffed shells

Taco/burrito fillings

Tofu

Turkey

Texturized vegetable protein (TVP)

Waffles

Things that don't freeze well include egg-based sauces, milk- or cream-based sauces (they separate but can be recombined after thawing), instant rice, raw salad ingredients, stuffed poultry, dishes with dried toppings, baked fruit pies, mayonnaise (unless it's mixed in or used as part of a sauce), cottage cheese, raw clams, hard-cooked eggs, and fried foods.

Cooking for Your Specific Diet

One of the most frequently asked questions I hear is, "What about vegetarians? How can vegetarians apply this method to how they eat?" Freezer cooking for vegetarians really isn't a problem. If you're making a meal, take a single serving out, freeze it, reheat it, and see how it turns out. If it turns out well, then you have a successful freezer meal to add to your Frozen Assets repertoire. I recommend this single-serving trial process for any meal you're not sure will freeze well. Tofu, TVP, and cooked dry beans all freeze well. Many people say they actually prefer the texture of pre-frozen tofu because it dries out a bit and becomes a little firmer after spending time in the freezer. You may also prepare many of the recipes without meat by omitting the meat altogether or substituting it with a meat replacement.

All of us eat differently. Each family prefers different foods. I don't necessarily recommend using either of my *Frozen Assets* books as your freezer meal bible. Don't feel you can only use the recipes in these books and never venture off and use your own recipes. Try several of the meal plans in the books to get started and get a feel for how the process works, but ultimately, I hope you will apply these methods to your own recipes and ways of eating.

Trial and Error

At times, this style of cooking can be a bit of a trial-and-error process. We all make occasional mistakes, but we learn from them and move on. I'll share with you some of the things I recommend watching for during meal preparation and planning. Feel free to learn from my experience.

Be sure to keep track of which meals you've used, and which ones are still in the freezer. A few times, I've forgotten to keep an accurate record, and at the end of the month, I found myself staring at four or five bags of spaghetti sauce with nothing else in the freezer for the last week of the month. My family and I didn't want to eat a full week of spaghetti-sauce meals, but that was all that was left. If you don't keep track, you may end up with a large amount of one type of meal, such as ground beef, tofu, or lasagna. By planning ahead and keeping track of the meals as you use them, you can space the meals for more of an assortment week by week. I recommend using a magnetic dry-erase board that can hang on the side of your refrigerator. Simply write down what you have put in your freezer, and cross each meal off as you use it. This makes it easy to get a quick grasp on what you have and what you need as you do your menu planning.

I've also had noodles completely disappear from my frozen soups. If you cook noodles until they're soft before freezing, they will disintegrate when thawed and reheated. To avoid this, wait until you're reheating the soup after freezing, and then throw in the noodles. The noodles will cook while the soup is reheating. Or, toss the raw noodles into the freezer bag with the soup just before placing the bag in the freezer.

Another tip to remember is to exhibit moderation at all times. I tend to stock up on meats and food items when they go on sale. One time, a friend called to let me know a local store was having a sale on ground turkey—forty pounds for $12. I ran down to the store and bought forty pounds of ground turkey. I was so proud of myself! $12? That's at least forty meals worth of meat, for a mere pittance. But six months later, we were still working our way through the ground turkey. My family likes ground turkey, but I discovered they didn't like forty pounds of it. If I had purchased ten pounds, I still would've had a wonderful bargain, and my family would've been much happier.

5
★ ★ ★

CREATING A
THIRTY-DAY MEAL PLAN

Remember, you don't *have* to do a full month of meals at once. You can choose to do mini sessions and stock up gradually, or you can do a week or two at a time. If you do want to prepare a full month of meals for the freezer at one time, here are the steps.

Step One

Choose Ten to Fifteen Recipes

First, choose your recipes, depending upon how often your family is willing to eat the same thing over the course of a month. Usually, I can get away with feeding my family the same thing three times during a month. So for my family's tastes and preferences, I could prepare ten different recipes, tripling each one for a month's worth of thirty meals. If your family will tolerate meals no more often than twice a month, you would need to choose fifteen different recipes for your month of meals. If your family will eat a particular meal no more frequently than once a month, you have a lot more work ahead of you, because you won't be doubling or tripling the recipes. You can prepare thirty completely different recipes, but that's a good deal harder and more time consuming. The fewer individual recipes you use, the better, as far as time, energy, and monetary expenditures for this type of cooking are concerned.

Step Two

Plan Your Meals for the Month

I try to make sure I spread the recipes apart during the month. My family might not be willing to eat the same meal three days in a row, but they're more than happy to eat the same meal if it's spread a week and a half apart. I can ensure meal spacing by taking a blank calendar page and filling it out ahead of time. First, I'll figure out what we're going to eat. I'll try to vary things—we want to have a certain number of chicken, ground beef, or vegetarian recipes, and I try to divide meals up accordingly over the course of the month. Otherwise, I might find that I've forgotten to make a variety of meals for the month, perhaps forgetting to make chicken recipes, or making a full month's worth of ground-beef meals.

Planning ahead really helps you schedule your recipes around what's on sale at the grocery store the week you'll be cooking. I also look through my freezer, refrigerator, and cupboards to see what I have on hand to use in the current meal plan.

Step Three

Make Your Shopping List

After you decide what you're going to make, go through your recipes and write down every single ingredient, along with the exact amounts of each that you'll need. Go through your cupboards, refrigerator, and freezer, checking off all ingredients you already have on hand and making certain you have the full amount needed. If you need four 16-ounce cans of tomato sauce, you should make sure that you actually have that total amount in ounces. If you only have two 8-ounce cans of sauce, you'll need to make a note about how many ounces of tomato sauce you still need to purchase.

After you've gone through all your supplies and cupboards, the items still remaining on your list of ingredients will be your shopping list.

Step Four

Gather Freezer Containers

You'll need to figure out what type of and how many freezer containers you'll need. You'll add these items to your shopping list as well. Take into account aluminum foil, disposable pans, plastic containers, plastic wrap, freezer bags (assorted sizes), labels, and marking pens.

Step Five

Prepare Your Refrigerator and Freezer

Before you head to the grocery store, you must thoroughly clean out your refrigerator and freezer to make room for all the food that you'll be bringing home from the market. It won't be in the refrigerator very long, because you'll be making it into prepared meals to freeze, but you don't want to find yourself staring at a full refrigerator while you're trying to unload multiple bags of groceries full of perishable food items.

If possible, you'll also want to turn the thermostat setting on your freezer to −10 degrees 24 hours before adding large amounts of unfrozen food to your freezer.

Step Six

Put Away Perishables First

Put away all of your perishables, but leave on the counter your canned goods and anything that doesn't need to be refrigerated overnight. Putting canned goods away just to take them out again in the morning is definitely inefficient. Trust me, you will appreciate any steps saved on that big cooking day.

Step Seven

Separate Your Recipes

Separate your recipes according to main ingredients or main protein: chicken, ground beef, ham, dried beans, or other poultry. Plan on preparing your recipes in groups according to the main ingredients. Essentially, what you're doing on a big cooking day is a series of mini sessions. For example, you'll do all the chicken recipes at one time, all the ground-beef recipes next, and then all your dried-bean recipes.

Step Eight

Prepare Ahead

Assemble all necessary utensils ahead of time: pots, pans, measuring cups, measuring spoons, stirring spoons, wire whisks, appliances, bakeware, freezer containers, and all others. It's a good idea to have two complete sets of measuring spoons and measuring cups—one for dry ingredients, and the other for wet.

Look through your recipes and break them down into individual steps. You'll want to group similar steps together: brown all the ground beef, chop all the vegetables, prepare and bone all the chicken, and cook all the beans. You don't want to have four or five little sessions of browning ground beef as you cook through your different menus; instead, do it all together at one time.

I find doing many of those things the night before the big cooking day is very helpful. In an hour and a half, I can quickly prepare spaghetti sauce, brown the ground beef, cook the chicken, chop the onions and celery, and grate any cheeses. It saves a great deal of time and effort for the next day.

Plan to prepare your most complicated recipes first thing in the morning, while you're still fresh. If you have anything that's time consuming or requires a lot of thought or quick movement, get it done before you move on to easier recipes.

Step Nine

Take Care of Yourself

Cooking for a month can be a tiring proposition. It's a long day, and it's a lot of work, but it won't be unbearable if you take simple steps to care for yourself.

Remember to think about your comfort and energy level as you go through the day. Get a good night's sleep the night before. Dress comfortably. Wear the most supportive shoes you have; good choices are nurses' or waitresses' footwear. Some people even wear hiking boots on cooking day. Don't cook barefoot. Tie back long hair, or wear a hairnet. Put on an apron, even if you don't usually wear one. If you're ever going to make a big mess in the kitchen, this will be the day.

Make it fun: Play upbeat music, sing, dance, and remember to smile.

Be sure to eat breakfast in the morning. Remember to stop for lunch, and actually sit down while you eat it! I can get so involved with the cooking process, I forget to eat all day. Take frequent minibreaks. Pull up a high stool next to the counter so you can sit down often. Do as much meal preparation as possible while sitting at the kitchen table.

Step Ten
Keep It Clean
Fill a sink with hot, soapy water so you can wash your pots and pans and measuring utensils as you go. Wash your hands frequently, especially after handling raw meats. Tuck a kitchen towel into the waistband of your apron so it's handy for quickly mopping up messes and spills.

Step Eleven
Avoid Overcooking
To prevent overcooking or that warmed-over taste, slightly undercook foods to be reheated after freezing. For example, if you're preparing a lasagna that requires a one-hour baking time, cut the time down to 50 minutes and cool and freeze the lasagna at that point. The meal will get its last ten minutes of cooking time during the reheating process. If you cook things all the way and then freeze and reheat them, you'll feel like you're eating leftovers. Overcooked food will start tasting warmed over, rather than fresh.

Step Twelve
Package, Label, and Freeze Your Food
Pack food in quantities for family-sized meals. You may also want to consider packing single-serving sizes for quick lunches. I have a friend whose husband travels three to five days a week. She prepares individual lasagnas so she can enjoy home-cooked meals when she is alone.

Cool food quickly before placing it in the freezer. Sometimes the quality of the food will suffer if the food isn't room temperature or cooler when the freezing process begins. The longer it takes for a food item to freeze completely, the bigger the ice crystals will be in the finished product. You can cool food by putting it into the refrigerator for a while, or fill the bottom of your sink with ice water and set the pans in the water until the food has cooled (stir the food to cool it more quickly). Some people who live in areas where it snows and gets below freezing during the winter will actually cool their food by placing it outside in a snow bank.

Do not put hot food directly into plastic freezer bags.

Pack your freezer containers tightly, without air pockets, but remember to leave head space of at least 1 inch to allow for the expansion of liquid-based meals.

Set meal packages directly onto freezer shelves, allowing room for air circulation. After the meals are frozen solid, stack them tightly.

Remove air from your freezer bags by either pressing the air out with your hands, starting at the bottom and working upward, or by using a drinking straw to suck out excess air before sealing.

Label all freezer bags and containers with the name of the meal, the date when it was frozen, the number of servings, heating instructions, and any other special preparation instructions, such as "sprinkle with 1 cup grated cheese before baking."

Package grated cheese or crumb toppings in small freezer bags, tape them to the main dish container, and include instructions on the label for adding the topping before reheating.

PREPARING YOUR KITCHEN

A kitchen filled with a minimum amount of high-quality, multipurpose items is easier to care for than a kitchen overflowing with single-use, low-quality items. The following is a list of kitchen supplies handy for a big cooking day.

Must-Haves

Apron

Baking dishes, 9-inch square, 9- × 13-inch, and 9-inch loaf pan)

Baking sheets, two

Bowls (several of various sizes for holding ingredients during preparation)

Bulb baster

Cake pans (two 8-inch rounds, two 8-inch squares)

Can opener (high-quality hand or electric)

Casserole dishes with covers, 2-quart and 3-quart

Colander

Corkscrew

Cutting board

Grater

Hot pads, at least two

Ladles, at least two

Kitchen scissors

Kitchen towels, several

Knives, 8-inch chef's knife, paring knife, and long serrated bread knife

Measuring cups, two complete sets— one for dry ingredients and one for wet ingredients

Measuring spoons, two complete sets

Mixing bowls, small, medium, and large

Muffin tins

Pastry brush

Pie pans
Rolling pin
Rubber gloves
Rubber spatulas, assorted sizes
Saucepans, one large, one medium
Scrub brush
Skillets, one large, one medium
Slotted spoons (made of reinforced nylon so they won't scratch pans)

Spoons, several wooden and also several long-handled stirring
Stockpot with lid, at least one
Tongs
Vegetable peeler
Vegetable steamer
Waterproof marking pen
Wire whisks, two different sizes

Helpful Tools

Blender
Electric mixer, hand-held or freestanding
Electric skillet
Electric wok
Food processor
Garlic press
Ice cream scoop, for making meatballs and scooping cookie dough

Microwave oven
Pizza pan
Rice cooker
Salad shooter, for grating cheese
Slow cooker (having two can be helpful)
Teakettle
Toaster
Toaster oven

Odds and Ends

Cupcake liners
Foil, heavy-duty
Freezer bags (assorted sizes)
Napkins
Paper towels

Permanent marking pens
Plastic freezer containers in various sizes
Plastic wrap, clear
Wax paper

Pantry Supplies

Don't run out and buy all these items in one shopping trip. As you go through your regular shopping and cooking processes, you'll find you've already stocked many of these items. If you add one or two additional items to your shopping list each payday, you'll quickly develop a well-stocked pantry.

Allspice, ground

Almonds, whole, sliced, and slivered

Almond extract

Artichoke hearts, marinated

Artichoke hearts, plain

Baking chocolate, unsweetened

Baking mix, commercial

Baking powder

Baking soda

Basil

Bay leaves

Beans, canned and dried—black, kidney, pinto, white, and lentils

Beef broth, canned

Bouillon cubes or granules, chicken and beef

Breadcrumbs

Catsup

Cayenne, ground

Celery seed

Chicken, canned

Chicken broth, canned

Chili powder

Chili sauce

Chocolate chips (semi-sweet)

Cilantro, ground

Cinnamon, ground and sticks

Cloves, ground

Cloves, whole

Cocoa powder (unsweetened)

Coconut, shredded

Cooking spray, nonstick

Couscous

Cornmeal

Cornstarch

Corn syrup

Crackers, assorted

Croutons

Cumin, ground

Currants, dried

Curry powder

Dill

Dry milk

Egg noodles

Evaporated milk

Fennel

Flour, all-purpose and whole-wheat

Fruit, canned, such as peaches, pears, oranges, applesauce, mixed fruit

Garlic, minced

Garlic powder

Garlic salt

Gelatin and pudding mixes

Ginger

Gravy mix packets

Green chiles

Herb blend

Honey

Hot chocolate mix, instant

Italian seasoning mix

Jams and jellies, assorted

Lemon peel

Lemon juice

Lemon pepper

Lime juice

Mace, ground

Maple extract

Maple syrup

Marjoram

Mayonnaise

Mint extract

Mushrooms, canned (whole and sliced)

Mustard, regular and Dijon-style

Mustard, dry

Nutmeg

Nuts, such as walnuts (halves, chopped, and whole), almonds, cashews, and pecans

Oatmeal, instant

Oats, rolled

Olive oil

Olives, black, whole and sliced, and green

Onion powder

Onion salt

Oregano

Paprika

Parmesan cheese, grated

Parsley flakes

Pastas, assorted dried, such as spaghetti, fettuccine, manicotti shells, elbow macaroni, bow ties, penne, rigatoni, small shells, and large shells

Peanut butter

Peanuts, in shell and shelled

Pectin

Pepper, black and white

Peppercorns, whole

Pepper sauce, hot

Pine nuts

Pizza sauce

Poppy seeds

Raisins

Red pepper flakes

Rice, brown, instant, and long-grain

Rice, wild

Rosemary

Saffron

Sage

Salad dressing mix packets

Salsa, mild, medium, or hot

Salt

Sesame oil

Sesame seeds

Sloppy joe seasoning packets

Soup, canned, such as tomato, chicken noodle, French onion

Soup, cream of mushroom, chicken, broccoli, and asparagus

Soup, dry mixes, such as chicken noodle and French onion

Soy sauce

Spaghetti sauce, jars or cans

Spaghetti sauce, mix packets

Sunflower seeds, shelled

Sugar, brown, granulated, and confectioners'

Sweetened condensed milk

Taco seasoning packets

Tarragon

Texturized vegetable protein (TVP)

Tomato juice

Tomato paste

Tomato sauce

Tomatoes, crushed or diced

Tomatoes, stewed (regular, diced, Italian-style, and Mexican-style)

Tomatoes, with green chiles

Thyme

Tuna

Turmeric, ground

Vanilla extract

Vegetables, assorted canned

Vegetable oil (same as cooking oil above)

Vegetable shortening (solid)

Vegetable broth, canned

Vegetable soup mix packets

Vinegar, balsamic, cider, red wine, white, and white wine

Water chestnuts

Wheat germ

Wine, dry red and dry white

Worcestershire sauce

Yeast, active dry

Refrigerator and Freezer Supplies

Butter

Buttermilk

Cheeses (Cheddar, Monterey Jack, mozzarella, Parmesan, ricotta, Romano, Swiss)

Corn kernels, frozen

Cottage cheese

Cream, whipping

Cream cheese

Eggs, large

Egg substitute

Garlic cloves, whole

Ginger, fresh, whole

Green beans, frozen

Lemon juice

Lima beans, frozen

Lime juice

Margarine

Milk

Mixed vegetables, frozen

Parmesan cheese, grated

Peas, frozen

Salad dressings, assorted

Sour cream

Tofu

Tortillas, corn and flour

Tortillas, flour

Yogurt, plain

Produce

Cabbage

Carrots

Celery

Cilantro, fresh

Garlic, heads of

Green onions

Bell pepper, green and red

Onions

Parsley, fresh

Potatoes

CHICKEN MINI SESSION #1

Chicken Fried Rice
Chicken Taco Sandwiches
Chicken Tortellini Soup

Chicken-Chili Mac
Lemon-Mushroom Chicken

Ingredients List

Meat

6 cups chicken, about two (3- to 4-pound) chickens, or 6 pounds chicken breasts

6 chicken cutlets or boneless chicken breasts

Dairy

2 large eggs

2 ounces reduced-fat Cheddar cheese

⅓ cup fat-free sour cream

4 ounces reduced-fat Monterey Jack cheese

Margarine

Bread and Pasta

6 French or kaiser rolls, split

1 cup dried cheese-filled tortellini

6 ounces dried elbow macaroni

Vegetables

3 medium onions

11 cloves garlic

Fresh ginger

1 medium zucchini

1 medium-sized red bell pepper

1 medium-sized green bell pepper

1 cup fresh snow peas

9 fresh asparagus spears

3 large carrots

2 celery stalks

1 head iceberg lettuce

2 cups sliced mushrooms

3 medium tomatoes

1 bunch fresh parsley

Canned/Boxed/Bottled

12 ounces long-grain rice

84 ounces canned fat-free chicken broth

⅓ cup salsa, medium or hot, to taste

2 (15-ounce) cans Mexican-style stewed tomatoes

1 (6-ounce) can red kidney beans

Seasonings and Staples

Cayenne, ground

Red pepper flakes

Soy sauce

Thyme

Black pepper

Bay leaf

White pepper

Oregano

Chili powder

Sugar

Cumin, ground

Flour, all-purpose

Nonstick cooking spray

Oriental sesame oil

Olive oil

Lemon juice

White wine, dry

Frozen

1 cup frozen corn kernels

Preparation Instructions

Chicken Prep

6 chicken breasts, uncooked: pound to ¼-inch thickness; keep covered in refrigerator until ready to use

3 cups cooked chicken breasts: cut into ½-inch pieces

3 cups cooked chicken breasts: shred

Boil the chicken pieces in a large Dutch oven or stockpot with enough water to fully cover the chicken. Add several stalks of celery and some sliced onion, if desired. Cook the chicken until the meat is white to the bone, and falls off the bone easily. Cool the cooked chicken slightly, and refrigerate overnight to cool completely. Skim fat off the chicken stock using a slotted spoon. Remove the chicken from the stock, saving the stock to make soup later. Bone the chicken.

Vegetable Prep

  3 medium onions: chop

  1 medium zucchini: slice into ½-inch pieces

  1 cup green bell pepper: chop

  1 cup red bell pepper: chop coarsely

  1 cup snow peas: remove stem ends and strings and cut into 1-inch pieces.

  1 cup thinly sliced carrots

  ½ cup thinly sliced celery

  2 cups sliced fresh mushrooms

  9 asparagus spears: cut into ½-inch pieces

  11 cloves garlic: mince

  2 teaspoons minced fresh ginger

Cheese Prep

  4 ounces (1 cup grated) reduced-fat Monterey Jack cheese

Odds and Ends Prep

  12 ounces long-grain white rice: cook according to package directions.

  6 ounces dried elbow macaroni: cook according to package directions. Set in large pan of cold water and store in refrigerator until ready to use.

Note: Place vegetables, meats, and cheeses into separate covered bowls or plastic bags, and refrigerate until ready to use.

Chicken Fried Rice

SERVES 6

—◆◆◆—

1½ cup diced onion

2 teaspoons minced fresh ginger

3 cloves garlic, minced

⅛ teaspoon red pepper flakes

2 tablespoons Oriental sesame oil

1 medium zucchini, sliced into
 ½-inch pieces

1 cup coarsely chopped red bell pepper

1 cup cut-up snow peas, stem ends
 and strings removed

9 asparagus spears, cut into ½-inch
 pieces

2 eggs, beaten

1 tablespoon vegetable oil

2 cups cooked, cubed chicken breast

12 ounces long-grain white rice,
 cooked and cooled

5 tablespoons soy sauce

Advanced Prep

Cook chicken in large pot of water the night before. Cube the cooked chicken. Cook the rice the night before. Store the chicken and rice in separate containers in the refrigerator until ready to use. Chop onions and red bell pepper. Mince ginger and garlic. Slice zucchini into ½-inch pieces. Remove strings from snow peas and cut into 1-inch pieces. Cut asparagus spears into ½-inch pieces.

Preparation

Heat the oil in a large wok or skillet over medium-high heat, and stir-fry the onions, ginger, garlic, and red pepper flakes for 2 minutes. Add the zucchini, bell pepper, snow peas, and asparagus. Stir-fry for 3 to 4 minutes more, or until the vegetables are just softened. Stir in the rice.

In separate pan, with the vegetable oil, scramble the eggs. Stir the eggs and chicken into the rice. Stir in the soy sauce and sesame oil. Cool. Spoon the mixture into a freezer bag. Label it, and freeze.

To Serve

Thaw the chicken mixture in the refrigerator at least 24 hours before serving.

To serve, heat 2 teaspoons vegetable oil in a large wok over medium-high heat, and stir-fry for 5 minutes, or until heated through.

Per Serving: 428 calories; 9.0g fat; 28.2g protein; 58.3g carbohydrates; 120mg cholesterol.

Chicken Taco Sandwiches

SERVES 6

1 cup chicken broth

3 cloves garlic, minced

1 teaspoon dried oregano leaves

1 teaspoon ground cumin

2 cups cooked shredded chicken
  breast

⅓ cup salsa (mild, medium, or hot)

6 French or kaiser rolls, split

For Serving Day

3 cups shredded iceberg lettuce

3 medium tomatoes, diced

2 ounces (½ cup grated) reduced-fat
  Cheddar cheese

⅓ cup fat-free sour cream

Advanced Prep

Cook chicken. Shred chicken meat. Mince garlic cloves.

Preparation

Boil 1 cup chicken broth with garlic, oregano, and cumin until reduced to ⅓ cup. Put the chicken and salsa into a mixing bowl, and stir the seasoned broth into it. Spoon the mixture into a freezer bag. Label it, and freeze. Wrap the rolls in foil, label them, and freeze.

To Serve

Thaw the chicken mixture in the refrigerator at least 24 hours before serving.

To serve, heat it in a microwave or in a saucepan over medium heat until hot.

Serve in French or kaiser rolls with hot chicken mixture, shredded lettuce, chopped tomatoes, grated cheese, and sour cream for garnish.

Per Serving: 278.0 calories; 7.3g fat; 24.7g protein; 25.6g carbohydrates; 56mg cholesterol.

Chicken Tortellini Soup

SERVES 6

6 cups reduced-fat chicken broth

1 cup thinly sliced carrots

½ cup chopped onions

½ cup thinly sliced celery

½ teaspoon dried thyme leaves

¼ teaspoon black pepper

1 bay leaf

1 cup cooked cubed chicken breast

1 cup dried cheese-filled tortellini

2 tablespoons sliced fresh parsley

Advanced Prep

Cook chicken; reserve broth. Cut chicken into ½-inch cubes. Slice carrots and celery. Chop onion.

Preparation

Bring the chicken broth to a boil, and add the carrots, onion, celery, thyme, black pepper, and bay leaf. Cover, reduce the heat to medium-low, and cook for 15 minutes. Cool. Remove the bay leaf. Stir in the chicken, pasta, and parsley. Spoon into freezer bags. Label them, and freeze.

To Serve

Thaw the chicken mixture in the refrigerator at least 24 hours before serving.

Heat it in a covered saucepan over medium heat for 15 minutes, or until the pasta is cooked.

Per Serving: 121.6 calories; 3.8g fat; 20.0g protein; 11.5g carbohydrates; 29mg cholesterol.

Chicken-Chili Mac

SERVES 6

1 cup chicken broth

1 cup chopped onions

1 cup chopped green bell peppers

2 tablespoons chili powder

2 cloves garlic, minced

¾ teaspoon ground cumin

½ teaspoon oregano

¼ teaspoon sugar

¼ teaspoon ground cayenne

2 (15-ounce) cans Mexican-style stewed tomatoes, chopped and undrained

1 cup frozen corn kernels, thawed

1 (6-ounce) can red kidney beans, drained

6 ounces dried elbow macaroni

7 ounces skinless and boneless chicken breasts, cooked and shredded

4 ounces (1 cup grated) reduced-fat Monterey Jack cheese (reserve ¼ cup)

Advanced Prep

Cook the chicken the night before. Shred the chicken. Cook noodles until just barely tender. Drain noodles, rinse in cold water, set in large pan of cold water, and store in refrigerator until ready to use.

Refrigerate cooked pasta in an airtight container for 3 to 5 days. You may add a little oil (1 to 2 teaspoons for each pound of cooked pasta) to help keep it from sticking. Because cooked pasta will continue to absorb flavors and oils from sauces, store cooked pasta separately from sauce. Chop the onion and green bell pepper. Grate the cheese. Mince garlic.

Preparation

Heat chicken broth over medium heat, and add the onion and green pepper, cooking until soft. Add the chili powder, garlic, cumin, oregano, sugar, and cayenne. Cook, stirring constantly, for 1 minute. Remove from the heat. Add the tomatoes, corn, and beans. Stir in the macaroni. Stir in the chicken and ¾ cup of the cheese. Cool.

Scoop into a freezer bag. Label it, and freeze. Put the remaining cheese in a separate freezer bag. Label it, and tape the bags together or place both bags together into another freezer bag. Seal, and freeze.

To Serve

Thaw the chicken mixture in the refrigerator at least 24 hours before serving. Preheat the oven to 350 degrees.

To serve, pour the mixture into a casserole, sprinkle with the remaining cheese, and bake for 25 minutes.

Per Serving: 323.2 calories; 6.8g fat; 32.1g protein; 33.4g carbohydrates; 58mg cholesterol.

Lemon-Mushroom Chicken

SERVES 6

6 chicken breasts	1½ cups reduced-fat chicken broth
9 tablespoons flour, divided	6 tablespoons lemon juice
1 tablespoon margarine	6 tablespoons dry white wine
1 tablespoon olive oil	1 tablespoon chopped parsley
2 cups sliced fresh mushrooms	½ teaspoon white pepper
3 cloves garlic, minced	

Advanced Prep

Pound the 6 chicken breasts to ¼-inch thick. Slice the mushrooms. Mince the garlic.

Preparation

Dredge the chicken breasts in flour, lightly coating both sides and reserving the remaining flour. Heat the margarine and oil in a 10-inch nonstick skillet over medium heat until the margarine is melted. Add the chicken, and cook over medium-high heat, turning once, until lightly browned, 2 to 3 minutes on each side. Transfer the chicken to a plate, and set aside. In the same skillet, sauté the mushrooms and garlic over medium-high heat until the mushrooms are soft, 1 to 2 minutes. Sprinkle with the reserved flour, and stir quickly to combine. Stir in the remaining ingredients, and bring to a boil. Reduce the heat to low, and cook , stirring frequently, until the mixture thickens and the flavors blend, 3 to 4 minutes. Return the chicken to the skillet, and cook until heated through, 1 to 2 minutes. Remove from the heat, and cool. Scoop into freezer bags. Label them, and freeze.

To Serve

Thaw the chicken mixture in the refrigerator at least 24 hours before serving.

To serve, pour the mixture into a nonstick skillet, and heat over medium heat until hot. Serve.

Per Serving: 168.6 calories; 6.0g fat; 12.2g protein; 15.2g carbohydrates; 18mg cholesterol.

★ ★ ★

CHICKEN
MINI SESSION #2

White Chicken Chili
Chicken-Asparagus
Crustless Quiche

Penne Cacciatore
Marinated Lime Chicken
Cheddar Chicken

Ingredients List

Meat

   7 pounds boneless chicken breasts

   6 whole chicken breast portions

   3 slices bacon

Dairy

   2½ cups skim milk

   3 large eggs

   10 ounces reduced-fat Cheddar cheese

   Parmesan cheese, grated

Bread/Pasta

   Dried egg noodles

   10 ounces (2 cups) dried penne pasta

Vegetables

   8 large asparagus spears

   1 medium-sized red bell pepper

   1 medium-sized green bell pepper

   3 medium onions

   5 limes

   1 bunch green onions

   1 large tomato

   4 cloves garlic

   1 bunch fresh cilantro

   ½ pound whole mushrooms

Canned/Boxed

   32 ounces fat-free chicken broth

24 ounces canned white beans

2 (4.5-ounce) cans chopped mild green chiles

2 (14 .5-ounce) cans diced tomatoes with Italian seasonings, undrained

Seasonings and Staples

Salt

Pepper

Cayenne, ground

Basil

Cumin, ground

Flour, all-purpose

Vegetable oil

Olive oil

White wine vinegar

Preparation Instructions

Chicken Prep

6 whole chicken breasts: leave these *whole and uncooked*; store in the refrigerator until ready to use.

6 pounds chicken breasts, cooked and cubed. To prepare, boil chicken pieces in a large Dutch oven or stockpot with enough water to fully cover the chicken. Add several stalks of celery and some sliced onion, if desired. Boil until meat is white to the bone and falls off the bone easily. After the chicken is finished cooking, cool slightly and place the pot in refrigerator to cool completely overnight. The fat will congeal on top of the pot, so you can easily scoop it away in the morning. After you've scooped off the fat, remove the chicken from the broth and debone it. Save the broth from the cooked chicken for using in recipes or making soup.

Vegetable Prep

3 medium onions: chop

2 cups asparagus: cut into 1-inch pieces

1 green bell pepper: slice thinly

½ cup red bell pepper: dice

¼ cup green onion: slice

1 tomato: seed and dice

4 cloves garlic: mince

5 limes: squeeze juice

¼ cup fresh cilantro: chop coarsely

1 (8-ounce) package whole mushrooms: halve

Cheese Prep

10 ounces reduced-fat Cheddar cheese: grate

Odds and Ends Prep

3 slices bacon: cook and crumble

1⅓ cups uncooked penne pasta: cook according to package directions until just tender. Rinse in cold water, place in large pan of cold water, and store in refrigerator until ready to use.

Note: Place vegetables, meats, and cheeses into separate covered bowls or plastic bags, and refrigerate until ready to use.

White Chicken Chili

SERVES 6

◆◗◆◖◆

1 cup reduced-fat chicken broth

2 medium onions, chopped

4 cloves garlic, minced

2 cups cooked, cubed chicken breast

1 (24-ounce) can canned white
    beans, drained

2 (4-ounce) cans chopped mild
    green chiles

1 teaspoon ground cumin

1½ teaspoon ground cayenne

Juice of 1 lime

¼ cup coarsely chopped fresh
    cilantro

Advanced Prep

Cook chicken meat; cut into ½-inch cubes. Chop onions. Mince garlic.

Preparation

Combine the broth, onions, and garlic in a large skillet over medium heat. Bring to a boil, and cook until the onions are soft. Remove from the heat, and cool.

Meanwhile, combine the chicken, beans, chiles, cumin, and cayenne in a large bowl. Gently stir in the onion mixture. Pour into a freezer bag. Label it, and freeze. In a small freezer bag, combine the lime juice and cilantro. Label it, attach it to the chili bag, and freeze.

To Serve

Thaw the meat mixture and the lime juice-cilantro mixture in the refrigerator at least 24 hours before serving.

To serve, heat the chicken chili mix in a large saucepan. Just before serving, stir in the lime juice and cilantro.

Per Serving: 277.0 calories; 3.2g fat; 29.1g protein; 33.8g carbohydrates; 49mg cholesterol.

Chicken-Asparagus Crustless Quiche

SERVES 6

⬥◆⬥

2 cups cut-up asparagus

2 teaspoons vegetable oil

½ cup diced red bell pepper

½ cup chopped onion

1 cup cooked, cubed chicken breast

½ teaspoon salt

¼ teaspoon black pepper

Pinch ground cayenne

1 cup skim milk

3 eggs, or 1 cup egg substitute

2 tablespoons all-purpose flour

4 ounces (1 cup grated) reduced-fat
cheddar cheese

Advanced Prep

Cook chicken; cut into ½-inch pieces. Chop bell pepper and onion. Cut asparagus spears into 1-inch pieces. Grate cheese.

Preparation

Cook the asparagus just until tender. Drain, and rinse. Heat the oil over medium-high heat, and sauté the red bell pepper and onion 5 minutes, or until soft. Remove from the heat. Stir in the chicken, salt, pepper, and cayenne. Whisk together the milk, eggs, and flour in a mixing bowl until foamy. Stir in the cheese, asparagus, and chicken mixture, mixing well. Spoon into a freezer bag. Label it, and freeze.

To Serve

Thaw the meat mixture and the lime juice in the refrigerator at least 24 hours before serving.

Preheat the oven to 350 degrees. Spray 9-inch pie plate or quiche pan with non-stick cooking spray.

To serve, squeeze the bag gently to recombine the quiche mixture. Pour quiche mixture into pie plate. Bake for 45 minutes, or until knife inserted near the center comes out clean. Let stand 10 minutes before serving. Slice into 6 equal wedge-shaped pieces.

Per Serving: 173.6 calories; 6.7g fat; 19.6g protein; 8.5g carbohydrates; 136mg cholesterol.

Penne Cacciatore

SERVES 6

1 small green bell pepper, thinly
   sliced

8 ounces whole mushrooms, cut in
   half

2 (14.5-ounce) cans diced tomatoes
   with Italian seasonings, undrained

1 cup reduced-fat chicken broth

2 cups cooked, cubed chicken breast

2 cups dried penne pasta, cooked
   and drained

For Serving Day

¼ cup grated Parmesan cheese

Advanced Prep

Cook chicken; cut into cubes. Slice green pepper. Halve mushrooms. Cook pasta according to package directions, until just tender. Rinse in cold water, place in large pan of cold water, and store in refrigerator until ready to use.

Preparation

Combine the broth, green bell pepper, mushrooms, and tomatoes in a large skillet, and cook over medium-high heat until the green pepper is tender and the mushrooms are cooked through. Remove from the heat. Stir in the chicken and pasta. Pour into a freezer bag. Label it, and freeze.

To Serve

Thaw the chicken mixture in the refrigerator at least 24 hours before serving.

To serve, reheat the mixture in a large skillet until heated through. Sprinkle with the Parmesan cheese, and serve hot.

Per Serving: 320 calories; 3.3g fat; 26.0g protein; 47.1g carbohydrates; 40mg cholesterol.

Marinated Lime Chicken

SERVES 6

Juice of 4 limes or 4 tablespoons
bottled lime juice

4 teaspoons white wine vinegar

½ cup plus 1 tablespoon olive oil

2 teaspoons dried basil

½ teaspoon salt

¼ teaspoon pepper

6 chicken breast portions, about 8
ounces each

Fresh basil sprigs, for garnish
if desired

Advanced Prep

None required for this recipe.

Preparation

Pour the lime juice into a mixing bowl Stir in the vinegar, olive oil, basil, salt, and pepper. Place chicken breast portions into a freezer bag. Pour lime sauce over top. Label it, and freeze.

To Serve

Thaw the chicken mixture in the refrigerator at least 24 hours before serving. Preheat the oven to 350 degrees.

To serve, heat the marinade in a small saucepan until it boils. Put the chicken pieces in an ovenproof dish, and pour the marinade over top. Bake in for 35 to 40 minutes, or until the chicken is tender and cooked through. Serve hot, sprinkled with fresh basil sprigs, if desired.

Per Serving: 191.8 calories; 4.1g fat; 32.8g protein; 6.2g carbohydrates; 81mg cholesterol.

Cheddar Chicken

SERVES 6

————————◆◖◆◗◆————————

1½ cups skim milk

1½ cups fat-free chicken broth

3 tablespoons all-purpose flour

6 ounces reduced-fat cheddar cheese,
    grated

2 cups cooked, cubed chicken

¼ cup sliced green onions

½ cup seeded, diced tomato

3 slices bacon, cooked and crumbled

For Serving Day

Egg noodles to serve 6, cooked

Advanced Prep

Cook chicken; cut into ½-inch cubes. Slice green onions. Cook and crumble bacon. Seed and dice tomato. Grate cheddar cheese.

Preparation

Mix together the milk, broth, and flour in a large saucepan. Heat over medium heat, stirring constantly, until the sauce thickens. Add the cheese, and stir until it melts. Add the chicken, green onions, tomatoes, and bacon. Cool. Pour into freezer bags. Label them, and freeze.

To Serve

Thaw the chicken mixture in the refrigerator at least 24 hours before serving.

To serve, reheat the chicken in a large saucepan over medium-low heat until heated through. Serve over hot noodles.

Per Serving: 349.3 calories; 5.0g fat; 29.0g protein; 48.0g carbohydrates; 94mg cholesterol.

CHICKEN
MINI SESSION #3

Cheese-and-Chicken Shells
Spiced Chicken Sandwiches
Artichoke-Chicken Bake

Chicken Enchiladas
Chicken-Mushroom Rolls
Chicken-Broccoli Noodles

Ingredients List

Meat
   24 boneless chicken breast halves

Dairy
   3 large eggs
   1¾ cups skim milk
   Fat-free mayonnaise
   3 cups fat-free sour cream
   Margarine
   ½ cup fat-free cottage cheese or ricotta
   2 ounces reduced-fat mozzarella
      cheese, grated
   4 ounces reduced-fat Swiss cheese

   3-ounce package fat-free cream
      cheese
   4 ounces reduced-fat Cheddar cheese

Bread/Pasta
   12 jumbo shell
   6 soft sandwich rolls, split
   6 (6-inch) flour tortillas
   10 ounces dried broad egg noodles

Vegetables
   2 large carrots
   4 cloves garlic

3 medium tomatoes

1 red onion

1 small green bell pepper

2 medium onions

2 celery stalks

1 bunch green onions

1 bunch fresh cilantro

3 cups broccoli florets

2 cups sliced mushrooms

Canned/Boxed

4 ½ cups fat-free chicken broth

1 (14-ounce) can water-packed artichoke hearts, drained and halved

½ cup salsa, mild, medium, or hot,
according to taste

1 (10¾ ounce) can 98-percent fat-
free cream of chicken soup

2 ounces onion- and garlic-flavored
croutons

Seasonings and Staples

Flour, all-purpose

Cornstarch

Nutmeg, ground

Cumin, ground

Parsley

Garlic powder

Salt

Pepper

Thyme

Paprika

Cayenne, ground

½ cup sliced almonds

1¼ cups dry white wine or apple
juice

Vegetable oil

Lemon juice

Preparation Instructions

Chicken Prep

6 whole *uncooked* chicken breast portions: pound breasts with meat mallet until very thin.

6 whole *cooked* chicken breast portions: leave these whole after cooking. To prepare, boil chicken pieces in a large Dutch oven or stockpot with enough water to fully cover the chicken. Add several stalks of celery and some sliced onion, if desired. Boil until meat is white to the bone and falls off the bone easily. After the chicken is finished cooking, cool slightly and place the pot in the refrigerator to cool completely overnight. The fat will congeal on top of the pot, so you can easily scoop it away in the morning. After you've scooped off the fat, remove the chicken from

the broth and de-bone. Save the broth from the cooked chicken for using in recipes or making soup.

3 cups of cooked chicken meat: shred

2 cups of cooked chicken meat: cut into strips

Remaining cooked chicken meat: chop in ½-inch pieces

Vegetable Prep

1½ cups onion: chop

½ cup green onions: slice thinly

½ cup carrot: grate

½ cup celery: chop

½ cup green bell pepper: chop

4 cloves garlic: mince

¼ cup fresh cilantro: mince

3 cups fresh broccoli: cut into bite-sized pieces, steam until just tender, and rinse with cold water.

2 cups fresh mushrooms: slice

Cheese Prep

2 ounces (½ cup) reduced-fat mozzarella cheese: grate

4 ounces (1 cup) reduced-fat Swiss cheese: grate

4 ounces (1 cup) reduced-fat Cheddar cheese: grate

Odds and Ends Prep

12 jumbo shells: cook according to package directions. Rinse in cold water to stop cooking process. Place in large pan of water in refrigerator until ready to use.

Cheese-and-Chicken Shells

SERVES 6

1 egg, beaten

½ cup fat-free cottage cheese or fat-free ricotta cheese

1 cup cooked, shredded chicken

2 ounces (½ cup grated) reduced-fat mozzarella cheese

½ cup grated carrot

1 clove garlic, minced

¼ teaspoon salt

Pepper, to taste

12 dried jumbo pasta shells, cooked and cooled

1¾ cups skim milk

2 tablespoons cornstarch

4 ounces (1 cup grated) reduced-fat Swiss cheese

⅛ teaspoon ground nutmeg

Advanced Prep

Cook chicken; shred (for total of 1 cup). Cook pasta shells according to package directions. Rinse in cold water to stop the cooking process. Grate mozzarella and Swiss cheeses. Grate carrots.

Preparation

Combine the egg, cottage cheese, chicken, mozzarella, carrot, garlic, salt, and pepper in a mixing bowl, stirring together well. Spoon the mixture into the pasta shells. Combine the milk and cornstarch in a saucepan; cook and stir until thickened and bubbly. Add the Swiss cheese and nutmeg, and stir until the cheese is melted. Arrange the stuffed shells on a freezer-proof pan. Spoon the sauce evenly over the shells. Wrap the pan with foil. Label it, and freeze.

To Serve

Thaw the chicken mixture in the refrigerator at least 24 hours before serving.

Preheat the oven to 350 degrees.

To serve, bake for 30 minutes, or until heated through. Sprinkle with nutmeg.

Per Serving: 341 calories; 4.5g fat; 21.7g protein; 52.0 carbohydrates; 51mg cholesterol.

Spiced Chicken Sandwiches

SERVES 6

¼ cup fat-free mayonnaise

½ teaspoon ground cumin

½ teaspoon garlic powder

½ teaspoon salt

½ teaspoon pepper

½ teaspoon dried thyme

¼ teaspoon paprika

Pinch ground cayenne

1 pound skinless boneless chicken breasts, cooked and cut into strips

1 cup reduced-fat chicken broth

6 soft rolls, split

For Serving Day

2 medium tomatoes, sliced

½ cup thinly sliced red onion

Advanced Prep

Cook chicken breasts in stockpot; cool and cut into strips.

Preparation

Stir the mayonnaise with the cumin, garlic powder, salt, black pepper, thyme, paprika and cayenne. Place chicken strips into labeled freezer bag; pour the chicken broth over the chicken strips; seal. Put the mayonnaise mixture into a plastic container, and cover it. Put the chicken bag, the mayonnaise mixture container, and the rolls into a large freezer bag. Label it, and freeze.

To Serve

Thaw the chicken mixture in the refrigerator at least 24 hours before serving.

To serve, heat the chicken slices and broth in a large skillet over medium heat until heated through. Meanwhile, split the rolls, and spread them with the mayonnaise mixture. Pour off excess broth, and divide the chicken evenly among the rolls. Layer them with the tomato and onion slices, and top with the other half of the roll. Serve warm.

Per Serving: 201.2 calories; 2.5g fat; 19.7g protein; 25.6g carbohydrates; 35mg cholesterol.

Artichoke-Chicken Bake

6 SERVINGS

¼ cup butter or margarine

1 cup chopped onions

1 clove garlic, minced

2 tablespoons all-purpose flour

¼ teaspoon salt

1¼ cup dry white wine or apple juice

1 cup reduced-fat chicken broth

1 (3-oz) package fat-free cream cheese

6 boneless and skinless chicken breasts, cooked and cooled

1 (14-ounce) can water-packed artichoke hearts, drained and halved

For Serving Day

½ cups sliced almonds

2 tablespoons chopped parsley

Advanced Prep

Cook chicken in stockpot. Remember to keep these 6 chicken pieces whole after cooking (don't cut or shred). Chop onion. Mince garlic.

Preparation

Melt the butter in a large skillet over medium heat, and sauté the onion and garlic until soft. Stir in the flour and salt until smooth. Cook 1 minute, stirring constantly. Add the wine and broth, and cook over medium heat, stirring constantly, until the mixture is thickened and bubbly. Add the cream cheese, stirring until the cheese melts. Remove from the heat, and set aside. Place the chicken breasts into a 2-quart casserole dish, and arrange the artichoke hearts over top. Spoon the cream-cheese mixture over the chicken and artichokes, and wrap the dish in foil. Label it, and freeze.

To Serve

Thaw the chicken mixture in the refrigerator at least 24 hours before serving.

Preheat the oven to 350 degrees.

To serve, bake the chicken for 35 minutes, or until bubbly. Sprinkle with the almonds and parsley, and serve.

Per Serving: 382.3 calories; 14.7g fat; 41.3g protein; 15.5g carbohydrates; 82mg cholesterol.

Chicken Enchiladas

6 SERVINGS

2 cups cooked, shredded boneless chicken breasts

2 cups fat-free sour cream

½ cup thinly sliced green onions

¼ cup minced fresh cilantro

½ teaspoon ground cumin

½ teaspoon salt

¼ teaspoon garlic powder

4 ounces (1 cup grated) reduced-fat cheddar cheese

6 (6-inch) flour tortillas

For Serving Day

½ cup salsa (mild, medium, or hot)

½ cup chopped tomato

Fresh cilantro sprigs, for garnish

Advanced Prep

Cook chicken in stockpot; shred cooked chicken meat. Grate cheddar cheese. Slice green onions. Mince cilantro.

Preparation

Combine the shredded chicken, sour cream, green onions, cilantro, cumin, salt, and garlic powder in a large bowl, mixing well. Spoon the chicken mixture into a freezer bag. Put the grated cheese into a small freezer bag. Label them, and put them into a large freezer bag with the tortillas. Label it, and freeze.

To Serve

Thaw the chicken mixture in the refrigerator at least 24 hours before serving.

Preheat the oven to 350 degrees. Spray a 9 × 13-inch baking pan with nonstick cooking spray.

To serve, assemble the enchiladas by placing the tortillas in a single layer on a flat surface. Divide the chicken mixture evenly among the 6 tortillas. Fold the sides of the tortillas over to enclose the filling. Place folded tortillas seam-side down into the prepared pan. Sprinkle them with the grated cheese, and cover the pan tightly. Cover tightly; Bake for 25 minutes, or until the filling is hot and the cheese is melted. Spoon the salsa over the enchiladas, sprinkle with chopped tomato, and garnish with fresh cilantro sprigs.

Per Serving: 261.4 calories; 4.5g fat; 24.7g protein; 31.0g carbohydrates; 40mg cholesterol.

Chicken-Mushroom Rolls

SERVES 6

———◆◈◆———

4 teaspoons margarine, divided

½ cup chopped onion

½ cup chopped celery

½ cup chopped green bell pepper

2 cloves garlic, minced

2 cups sliced mushrooms

4 teaspoons all-purpose flour

1 cup reduced-fat chicken broth

1 teaspoon lemon juice

2 ounces onion- and garlic-flavored croutons

2 eggs, beaten

6 boneless chicken breasts, pounded thin

Advanced Prep

Pound chicken breasts with meat mallet until very thin. Chop onion, celery, and green pepper. Slice mushrooms. Mince garlic.

Preparation

Heat 2 teaspoons margarine in a large skillet over medium heat, and sauté the onion, celery, green pepper, and garlic until softened. Remove from the heat. In another skillet, heat the remaining 2 teaspoons margarine, and cook the mushrooms until softened, stirring frequently. Sprinkle the flour over the mushrooms, and stir to combine. Continue cooking and stirring over medium heat for 1 minute. Add the broth and lemon juice, and cook for 2 minutes, stirring frequently. Remove from the heat. Stir the croutons and eggs into the onion mixture. Spread the mixture onto the center of each chicken breast, and wrap the chicken breast around the filling. Secure each chicken roll with a toothpick, and place each seam-side down in a 9 × 13-inch baking dish. Wrap the dish in foil. Label it. Pour the mushroom sauce into a freezer bag, attach it to the chicken roll pan, and freeze.

To Serve

Thaw the chicken mixture in the refrigerator at least 24 hours before serving.

Preheat the oven to 350 degrees.

To serve, stir the mushroom sauce to recombine it. Add a small amount of water or chicken broth if it is too thick. Pour the mushroom sauce over the chicken rolls, and cover the pan tightly. Bake for 45 minutes, or until the chicken is cooked through.

Per Serving: 284.1 calories; 8.1g fat; 39.5g protein; 13.8g carbohydrates; 153mg cholesterol.

Chicken-Broccoli Noodles

SERVES 6

1½ cups fat-free chicken broth

1 cup fat-free sour cream

1 (10 ¾-ounce) can 98-percent fat-free cream of chicken soup

6 boneless and skinless chicken breasts, cut into ½-inch pieces

3 cups fresh broccoli florets

For Serving Day

10 ounces (3½ cups) dried broad egg noodles

Advanced Prep

Cook chicken in stockpot. Cut into ½-inch pieces. Cut up broccoli and steam until just tender. Rinse with cold water.

Preparation

Combine the chicken broth, 1½ cups water, sour cream, and chicken soup in a mixing bowl. In a second bowl, insert the chicken pieces and broccoli, and pour the soup mixture over the top. Stir gently to combine. Spoon into a large freezer bag. Label it, and freeze.

To Serve

Thaw the chicken mixture in the refrigerator at least 24 hours before serving.

To serve, cook the noodles according to manufacturer's directions. Reheat the chicken in a large skillet over medium heat, stirring frequently, until heated through. Ladle over hot noodles.

Per Serving: 387.7 calories; 4.4g fat; 46.1g protein; 41.8g carbohydrates; 132mg cholesterol.

10

CHICKEN
MINI SESSION #4

Old-Fashioned Chicken
*   and Rice*
Chicken Vegetable Skillet
Chicken Pasta Italiano

Chicken Noodle Soup
Mushroom-Chicken
*   Couscous*

Ingredients List

Meat
   6 pounds boneless and skinless
      chicken breasts

Dairy
   Margarine
   Parmesan cheese, grated
   2 cups skim milk

Bread/Pasta
   1½ cups long-grain white rice
   6 ounces dried bow-tie pasta

5 ounces dried broad egg noodles
1 ½ cups couscous

Vegetables
   6 large onions
   1 bunch fresh parsley
   14 cloves garlic
   1 small green bell pepper
   2 small red bell pepper
   1 bunch fresh cilantro
   4 large carrots
   1 large celery rib

1 pound potatoes

3 medium tomatoes

2 small zucchini

12 ounces fresh mushrooms

Canned/Boxed

11½ cups canned fat-free chicken broth

1 (6-ounce) jar sliced mushrooms

1 (16-ounce) can Italian-style stewed tomatoes

Seasonings and Staples

Poultry seasonings

Thyme

Salt

Pepper

Italian seasoning

Cornstarch

Cayenne, ground

Olive oil

Vegetable oil

Nonstick cooking spray

Cooking sherry

Soy sauce

White vinegar

Frozen

½ cup frozen peas

Preparation Instructions

Chicken Prep

4½ pounds boneless and skinless chicken breasts—cut into 1-inch cubes.

1 pound chicken breasts—slice into ½-inch strips.

1 pound chicken breasts—place between sheets of plastic wrap or wax paper; pound with meat mallet until ¼-inch thick; cut into ½-inch wide strips.

Vegetable Prep

6 cups onions: chop

½ cup celery: chop

3 medium tomatoes: seed and chop

½ cup fresh parsley: chop

1 small green pepper: chop

2 small zucchini: slice thinly

4 large carrots: slice thinly

½ pound fresh mushrooms: slice

2 small red bell peppers: cut into strips

14 cloves garlic: mince

1 pound potatoes: peel and slice thinly. Place potatoes in a large bowl of cold water with 1 teaspoon white vinegar or lemon juice. Refrigerate until ready to use; dry thoroughly before adding to skillet when preparing recipe.

Old-Fashioned Chicken and Rice

SERVES 6

2½ cups fat-free chicken broth

1½ pounds boneless and skinless chicken breasts, cut into 1-inch pieces

1 cup chopped onions

6 cloves garlic, minced

¼ cup minced fresh parsley

1 small red bell pepper, sliced into thin strips

1½ cups long-grain rice, uncooked

1 (6-ounce) jar sliced mushrooms, undrained

1 teaspoon poultry seasonings

Advanced Prep

Cut up chicken into 1-inch pieces. Chop onions. Mince garlic cloves and parsley. Slice red bell pepper into long, thin strips.

Preparation

Bring the broth to a boil over medium-high heat in a large saucepan or Dutch oven. Add the remaining ingredients, mix well, and return to a boil. Reduce the heat to medium, cover tightly, and cook 20 minutes or until the chicken is no longer pink and the rice is tender. Cool. Place the mixture into freezer bags. Label them, and freeze.

To Serve

Thaw the chicken mixture in the refrigerator at least 24 hours before serving.

To serve, reheat the chicken in a large skillet over medium heat, stirring frequently, until heated through.

Per Serving: 301.9 calories; 1.7g fat; 30.2g protein; 43.3g carbohydrates; 53mg cholesterol.

Chicken Vegetable Skillet

SERVES 6

3 tablespoons olive or vegetable oil

1 pound potatoes, thinly sliced and soaked in water with 1 teaspoon white vinegar

1 pound boneless and skinless chicken breasts, cut into 1-inch cubes

3 tablespoons butter or margarine

1 cup chopped onion

1 cup chopped green bell pepper

1 cup sliced carrot

3 cloves garlic, minced

1 (15-ounce) can Italian-style stewed tomatoes, chopped and undrained

3 tablespoons chopped fresh parsley

½ teaspoon dried thyme

½ teaspoon salt

½ teaspoon pepper

Advanced Prep

Cut chicken into 1-inch cubes. Chop onion and green pepper. Slice carrots. Mince garlic. Peel and thinly slice potatoes; place potatoes in a large bowl of cold water with 1 teaspoon white vinegar or lemon juice. Refrigerate potatoes until ready to use; dry thoroughly before adding to skillet. Chop stewed tomatoes; reserve liquid.

Preparation

Heat the oil in a large skillet over medium-high heat. Thoroughly dry the potatoes and the chicken, and add them to the skillet. Cook, stirring constantly, until the chicken is no longer pink. Transfer the mixture to a separate container, and set aside. Using the same skillet, melt the butter over high heat, and sauté the onion, green pepper, carrot, and garlic until just barely tender. Add the potato–chicken mixture, and stir in the tomatoes, tomato liquid, and remaining spices. Reduce the heat to low, and cook, stirring frequently, until the potatoes are just barely starting to get tender, less than 5 minutes. Remove from the heat. Cool in refrigerator. Spoon the mixture into a freezer bag. Label it, and freeze.

To Serve

Thaw the chicken mixture in the refrigerator at least 24 hours before serving.

To serve, reheat the chicken in a large skillet over medium heat, stirring frequently.

Per Serving: 254.8 calories; 11.3g fat; 17.0g protein; 22.8g carbohydrates; 35mg cholesterol.

Chicken Pasta Italiano

SERVES 6

2 teaspoons olive oil

2 cloves garlic, minced

1 pound boneless chicken breasts, cut into ½-inch strips

1 cup chopped onions

1 small zucchini, sliced

1 small red pepper, cut into thin strips

½ cup frozen peas

1 teaspoon salt

1 teaspoon dried Italian seasoning

2 medium tomatoes, seeded and chopped

For Serving Day

6 ounces dried bow-tie pasta

⅛ cup grated Parmesan cheese, for serving

Advanced Prep

Seed and chop tomatoes. Chop onion. Slice zucchini. Cut red pepper into thin strips. Mince garlic. Cut chicken breasts into ½-inch strips.

Preparation

Heat the oil in a large skillet over medium heat, and sauté the garlic and chicken strips for 5 minutes. Add the onion, zucchini, red pepper, peas, salt, and Italian seasoning, and cook 1 minute longer. Remove from the heat, and stir in tomatoes. Cool. Spoon the mixture into freezer bags. Label them, and freeze.

To Serve

Thaw the chicken mixture in the refrigerator at least 24 hours before serving.

Cook the pasta according to manufacturer's directions. To serve, reheat the chicken in a large skillet over medium heat, stirring frequently, until heated through. Toss the chicken and pasta together, and garnish with the Parmesan cheese.

Per Serving: 197.7 calories; 3.1g fat; 13.0g protein; 29.6g carbohydrates; 19mg cholesterol.

Chicken Noodle Soup

SERVES 6

———◆◆◆———

1 teaspoon vegetable oil

2 cups chopped onions

8 cups reduced-fat chicken broth

3 cloves garlic, minced

½ teaspoon thyme

¼ teaspoon pepper

2 large carrots, sliced thinly

½ cup chopped celery

1 pound boneless chicken breasts, cut into 1-inch cubes

1 small zucchini, thinly sliced

1 medium tomato, seeded and chopped

2 tablespoons chopped parsley

5 ounces dried broad egg noodles

Advanced Prep

Cut chicken into ½-inch cubes. Chop onions, celery, and parsley. Seed and chop tomatoes. Mince garlic. Slice carrots.

Preparation

Heat the oil in a large saucepan or Dutch oven over medium heat, and sauté the onion until softened. Stir in the broth, garlic, thyme, pepper, carrots, celery, and chicken. Reduce the heat to low, cover, and cook until the carrots are just tender and the chicken is no longer pink, less than 10 minutes. Remove from the heat. Stir in the zucchini, tomato, and parsley. Cool. Spoon into a freezer bag. Label it, and freeze.

To Serve

Thaw the chicken mixture in the refrigerator at least 24 hours before serving.

To serve, place the chicken into a large saucepan or Dutch oven, and stir in the noodles. Heat over medium heat until the chicken is heated through and the noodles are tender.

Per Serving: 230.3 calories; 2.9g fat; 33.6g protein; 29.1g carbohydrates; 58mg cholesterol.

Mushroom-Chicken Couscous

SERVES 6

1 pound boneless and skinless
chicken breasts

2 teaspoons cornstarch

¼ cup reduced-fat chicken broth

2 tablespoons soy sauce

⅛ teaspoon cayenne

3 tablespoons sherry

1 tablespoon margarine

1 large onion, diced

½ pound mushrooms, sliced

For Serving Day

2 cups skim milk

¾ cup reduced-fat chicken broth

1½ cups couscous

Fresh cilantro sprigs (optional)

Advanced Prep

Place chicken between sheets of plastic wrap or wax paper. Pound with a meat mallet until ¼-inch thick. Cut chicken into ½-inch wide strips. Chop onion. Slice mushrooms.

Preparation

Stir together the cornstarch, ¼ cup broth, soy sauce, cayenne, and sherry in a large bowl. Heat the margarine in a large skillet or saucepan over medium-high heat, and sauté the onion and mushrooms, cooking until the onions turn golden brown. Remove from the heat. Remove the onion mixture from the skillet, and set aside. Spray the skillet with nonstick cooking spray, and heat it over medium-high heat. Sauté the chicken, stirring frequently, until the chicken is no longer pink. Add the onion–mushroom mixture and the cornstarch mixture, stirring constantly, and cook over medium-high heat until the sauce thickens and is bubbly. Remove from the heat. Cool. Spoon into a freezer bag. Label it, and freeze.

To Serve

Thaw the chicken mixture in the refrigerator at least 24 hours before serving.

To serve, stir the milk and remaining broth together in a large saucepan. Heat to boiling. Stir in the couscous, cover the pan, and remove from the heat; let sit for 10 minutes until liquid is absorbed. Heat the chicken mixture over medium heat in large skillet until heated through. Fluff the couscous. Serve the chicken with couscous, and garnish with the cilantro, if using.

Per Serving: 317.7 calories; 3.4g fat; 25.9g protein; 44.4g carbohydrates; 37mg cholesterol.

11
★ ★ ★

Turkey
Mini Session

Roast Turkey Dinner
Turkey-Potato Pie
Turkey Divan
Turkey-Spaghetti Bake

Turkey Tetrazzini
Turkey-Asparagus Strata
Turkey Soup
Turkey-Tortilla Casserole

Ingredients List

Meat

    1 whole turkey (weight determined
        by chart on page 75–76)

8 ounces low-fat Monterey Jack cheese

Parmesan cheese, grated

Sour cream

Dairy

    9 cups skim milk

    4 large eggs

    Butter

    Margarine

    8 ounces fat-free cream cheese

    4 ounces reduced-fat mozzarella cheese

    2 ounces reduced-fat Cheddar cheese

Bread/Pasta

    1¼ pounds dried spaghetti

    6 ounces elbow macaroni

    10 (6-inch) corn tortillas

    10 slices bread, white or whole wheat

Vegetables

    10 onions

1 large green bell pepper

9 celery stalks

8 large carrots

3 cups sliced fresh mushrooms

22 cloves garlic

1 bunch fresh parsley

1 cup sliced asparagus

2 bunches fresh spinach leaves

12 broccoli stalks

Canned/Boxed

6 cups fat-free chicken broth plus 1 cup broth per pound of meat (to freeze the turkey dinner)

2 packets instant beef broth and seasoning mix

Instant mashed potato flakes

24 ounces tomato sauce

1 (10-ounce) can tomatoes and green chiles

1 (7 ½-ounce) can whole tomatoes

Seasonings and Staples

Basil, dried

Bay leaves

Cilantro, dried

Salt

Black pepper

White pepper

Sage, dried

Thyme, dried

Flour, all-purpose

Paprika

1 bunch fresh parsley

2½ cups dry white wine

⅓ cup dry red wine

Olive oil

Vegetable oil

Dijon-style mustard

Frozen

2 cups frozen corn kernels

Preparation Instructions

Turkey Prep

1 whole turkey: prepare according to instructions in the Roast Turkey recipe. After roasting, cover it with foil, and refrigerate it overnight to cool completely. Slice the meat for the roast turkey meal. Remove the remaining meat, and cube it. Reserve the carcass for soup.

11 cups cooked cubed turkey meat

Vegetable Prep

4 medium onions: cut into quarters

6 medium onions: chop

9 celery stalks: cut into 2-inch pieces

4 medium carrots: cut into 2-inch pieces

4 medium carrots: slice thinly

1 large green bell pepper: chop

14 cloves garlic: mince

12 broccoli stalks: steam until just tender; rinse in cold water; and store, covered, in refrigerator until ready to use.

3 cups mushrooms: slice

2 bunches fresh spinach leaves: tear into small pieces

1 cup asparagus: slice thinly. In medium saucepan of boiling water, cook asparagus 3 minutes, until just tender. Drain, discard liquid, rinse under cold running water until cool, and drain again.

1 bunch fresh parsley, chop

Cheese Prep

4 ounces reduced-fat mozzarella cheese: grate

2 ounces reduced-fat Cheddar cheese: grate

8 ounces low-fat Monterey Jack cheese: grate

Odds and Ends Prep

1¼ pounds dried spaghetti: prepare according to package directions, cooking until just barely tender. Drain and rinse in cold water, and place cooked noodles in large bowl of cold water in refrigerator until ready to use.

Roast Turkey

You'll need a minimum 10-pound turkey for using in the turkey recipes. For the main roast turkey dinner, add ¾ pound per person to the 6 pounds already required for the other recipes.

Number of People = Weight of Turkey

6 people = 14½ pounds

8 people = 16 pounds

10 people = 17½ pounds

12 people = 19 pounds

14 people = 20½ pounds

16 people = 22 pounds

18 people = 23½ pounds

20 people = 25 pounds

To Prepare Turkey

3 onions, quartered

6 celery stalks, sliced

2 medium carrots, sliced

2 bay leaves

1½ cups white wine or water

Turkey, rinsed, dried, and giblets removed

1 tablespoon olive oil

2 teaspoons salt

2 teaspoons pepper

2 teaspoons dried sage

1 teaspoon dried thyme

Fat-free chicken broth, 1 cup per pound (reserve until time to freeze meat)

Preheat the oven (see roasting chart below).

Put 2 quartered onions, 4 celery stalks, carrots, bay leaves, and white wine in the bottom of a deep roasting pan. Stuff turkey loosely with the remaining onion and celery stalks. Mix the olive oil with the salt, pepper, sage, and thyme, and brush the turkey with the mixture. Cover turkey loosely with a large sheet of foil coated lightly with olive oil, crimping foil onto edges of roasting pan. Cook according to chart below. During last 45 minutes, cut band of skin or string between legs and tail. Uncover and continue roasting until done. Baste if desired.

Turkey Roasting Chart (turkey loosely wrapped with foil)

12 to 16 pounds / 325 degrees / 4 to 5 hours

16 to 20 pounds / 325 degrees / 5 to 6 hours

20 to 24 pounds / 325 degrees / 6 to 7 hours

Testing for Doneness

About 20 minutes before the end of the roasting time, test the turkey for doneness. The skin on the thickest part of the drumstick should feel soft when squeezed between your fingers, the drumstick should move freely, and the meat thermometer inserted into thickest part of leg should read 185 degrees.

Freezing Instructions

Pour all meat juices from the roasting pan into a bowl, and remove the vegetables. Chill the juices until the fat firms. Skim the fat off the turkey juices, using a slotted spoon. Pour the remaining juices into a freezer bag. Label it, and freeze. Allow the turkey to cool in the pan for about 30 minutes; refrigerate the turkey to cool it completely. When fully chilled, slice the turkey, removing all meat from the bones. Put the breast and dark meat into freezer bags, reserving 8 cups of diced turkey meat for the "leftover" recipes. Pour chicken broth into bags over the meat. Label them, and freeze.

Thaw a bag of meat and broth and a bag of turkey drippings in the refrigerator at least 24 hours before serving.
Preheat the oven to 350 degrees.

To serve, place the meat into a baking dish, cover it, and bake for 30 minutes. Alternatively, place the turkey and broth into a microwave-safe dish, cover it with plastic wrap, and heat according to manufacturer's directions. Drain off the broth, reserving it to make more gravy, if needed. Arrange the heated turkey slices attractively on a platter. Serve.

Gravy Instructions

Serves 12

If needed, add additional water, chicken broth, or white wine to equal 3 cups.

2 tablespoons butter or margarine   ½ teaspoon salt (optional)

½ cup white wine   3 cups thawed turkey drippings

⅓ cup all-purpose flour

Melt the butter in a saucepan over medium heat. Stir in the flour and salt, if using. Reduce the heat to medium-low, and cook until bubbly, stirring constantly. Slowly stir the turkey drippings into the butter mixture, and continue to stir while increasing the heat to medium. Cook until the mixture boils, and reduce the heat to low, stirring and cooking 2 minutes more.

Turkey Potato Pie

SERVES 6

———◆❖◆———

1 cup instant mashed potato flakes

1 tablespoon butter

3 cups boiling water

2 teaspoons vegetable oil

1½ cups chopped onions

3 cloves garlic, minced

2 cups cooked, cubed turkey meat

3 tablespoons all-purpose flour

⅓ cup dry red wine

2 packets instant beef broth and
   seasoning mix

3 tablespoons chopped fresh parsley

Advanced Prep

Cook and cube turkey meat. Chop onions. Mince garlic. Prepare potatoes: using fork, in medium bowl combine potato flakes, 2 cups boiling water, and the butter; mix until light and fluffy. Cool potatoes.

Preparation

Combine the instant potatoes with the butter and 2 cups boiling water, mixing until fluffy. Set aside to cool.

Heat the oil in a large skillet over high heat, and sauté the onion and garlic until soft, about 1 minute. Remove from the heat. Stir in the turkey, and sprinkle the flour over turkey mixture, stirring to combine. Return the skillet to the heat, reduce the heat to medium-high, and cook, stirring constantly, for 1 minute. Add ¾ cup water, the red wine, and the broth mix; cook until the mixture comes to a boil. Remove from the heat, and cool. Stir in the parsley. Place the turkey mixture and the potatoes into separate freezer bags. Label and seal both bags and place them into a large freezer bag. Label it, and freeze.

To Serve

Thaw the turkey and potatoes in the refrigerator at least 24 hours before serving.

Preheat the oven to 350 degrees.

To serve, put the turkey mixture into a 2-quart ovenproof dish, and top it with the potato mixture, spread evenly to cover. Bake for 20 to 30 minutes, or until the turkey is heated through and the potato topping is golden brown.

Per Serving: 297.8 calories; 13.0g fat; 18.9g protein; 25.2g carbohydrates; 53mg cholesterol.

Turkey Divan

6 SERVINGS

3 tablespoons margarine

⅓ cup flour

½ teaspoon salt

¼ teaspoon white pepper

3 cups skim milk

1 (8-ounce) package fat-free cream cheese, cut into small pieces

2 cups cooked, cubed turkey

12 broccoli stalks, steamed until tender

For Serving Day

6 slices white bread, toasted

¼ teaspoon paprika

Advanced Prep

Roast and cube turkey. Steam broccoli stalks until just tender; cool.

Preparation

Heat the margarine in a large skillet over medium-high heat, and stir in the flour, salt, and pepper. Cook, stirring constantly, until the mixture is bubbling, about 3 minutes. Gradually stir in the milk, and continue to stir and cook until the mixture thickens. Stir in the cream cheese, and cook, stirring constantly, until the cheese melts. Stir in the turkey pieces. Remove from the heat, and cool. Spoon the turkey and cheese mixture into a freezer bag. Label it. Place the steamed broccoli stalks into a separate freezer bag. Label it. Place both bags into a larger freezer bag. Label it, and freeze.

To Serve

Thaw the turkey mixture and the broccoli in the refrigerator at least 24 hours before serving.

Preheat the broiler.

To serve, pour the turkey mixture into a saucepan, and heat over low heat, stirring constantly, until heated through. Meanwhile, toast the bread, and place the slices in a roasting pan. Divide the broccoli stalks, and place them on top of each piece of toast. Pour the turkey mixture over top of the broccoli stalks, dividing it evenly. Sprinkle each lightly with paprika. Broil for about 1 minute, or until the cheese mixture is bubbling. Remove from the heat, and serve.

Per Serving: 314 calories; 9.7g fat; 32.1g protein; 29.4g carbohydrates; 48mg cholesterol.

Turkey-Spaghetti Bake

6 SERVINGS

2 tablespoons reduced-fat chicken broth

1½ cups chopped green bell pepper

1 cup chopped onion

6 cloves garlic, minced

2 cups cooked, cubed turkey

½ teaspoon salt

½ teaspoon pepper

3 cups tomato sauce

1 tablespoon basil

⅓ cup chopped fresh parsley

10 ounces dried spaghetti, cooked and cooled

4 ounces (1 cup grated) reduced-fat mozzarella cheese, grated

For Serving Day

Tomato slices, for garnish, if desired

Fresh basil, for garnish, if desired

Advanced Prep

Roast and cube turkey. Prepare spaghetti according to package directions until just barely tender; drain and rinse in cold water. Place cooked noodles in large bowl of cold water in refrigerator until ready to use. Chop green pepper and onion. Mince garlic. Grate mozzarella cheese.

Preparation

Spray a 9 × 13-inch baking pan with nonstick cooking spray. Heat the chicken broth in a large skillet, and add the bell pepper, onion, and garlic. Cook over medium-high heat, stirring frequently, until the vegetables are softened. Stir in the turkey, salt, pepper, and tomato sauce, and bring the mixture to a boil. Remove from the heat, and stir in the basil and parsley. Spread half of the spaghetti evenly over the bottom of the prepared pan; top with half the turkey mixture. Repeat the layers, sprinkling the cheese evenly over top. Cover the pan with foil. Label it, and freeze.

To Serve

Thaw the casserole in the refrigerator at least 24 hours before serving.

Preheat the oven to 350 degrees.

To serve, bake, covered, for 35 to 40 minutes, or until hot and bubbling. Garnish with fresh tomato slices and basil, if desired.

Per Serving: 366.1 calories; 4.8g fat; 30.8g protein; 50.5g carbohydrates; 40mg cholesterol.

Turkey Tetrazzini

SERVES 6

2 tablespoons reduced-fat chicken broth

3 cups sliced mushrooms

1 cup chopped onions

¼ teaspoon thyme

½ teaspoon salt

½ teaspoon pepper

4 tablespoons all-purpose flour

3 cups skim milk

1 cup fat-free chicken broth

½ cup dry white wine

2 cups cooked, cubed turkey

10 ounces dried spaghetti, cooked and cooled

3 tablespoons minced parsley

¼ cup grated Parmesan cheese

Advanced Prep

Roast and cube turkey. Slice mushrooms. Chop onion. Prepare spaghetti according to package directions until just barely tender; drain and rinse in cold water. Place cooked spaghetti in large bowl of cold water in refrigerator until ready to use.

Preparation

Spray 9 × 13-inch baking dish with nonstick cooking spray. Heat the reduced-fat chicken broth in a large skillet over medium heat, and add the mushrooms, onions, thyme, salt, and pepper. Cook, stirring frequently, until the mushrooms are golden brown, about 5 minutes. Stir in the flour, milk, and broth, and cook until slightly thickened, stirring constantly, about 1 minute. Remove from the heat. Stir in the wine. Put the turkey and spaghetti into a large bowl, and pour the mushroom mixture over top, tossing to combine. Transfer the mixture to the prepared dish, and sprinkle with parsley and Parmesan cheese. Cool. Cover with foil. Label it, and freeze.

To Serve

Thaw the casserole in the refrigerator at least 24 hours before serving.

Preheat the oven to 350 degrees.

To serve, bake, uncovered, for 25 to 35 minutes, and serve hot or until lightly browned and bubbling.

Per Serving: 395.8 calories; 3.8g fat; 34.9g protein; 53.8g carbohydrates; 37mg cholesterol.

Turkey-Asparagus Strata

SERVES 8

———◆◆◆———

2 tablespoons reduced-fat chicken
 broth

1 medium onion, chopped

3 cloves garlic, minced

2 cups cooked, cubed turkey

1 cup thinly sliced asparagus

10 slices of bread, white or whole
 wheat, crusts removed, cut into 4
 triangles each

3 cups skim milk

4 eggs

¼ cup all-purpose flour

1 teaspoon Dijon mustard

½ teaspoon salt

¼ teaspoon pepper

2 ounces (½ cup grated) reduced-fat
 Cheddar cheese

Advanced Prep

Cook and cube turkey meat. Mince garlic. Chop onion. Slice asparagus. Grate cheddar cheese. In medium saucepan of boiling water, cook asparagus 3 minutes, until just tender. Drain, discarding liquid; rinse under cold running water until cool.
Drain again.

Preparation

Spray 9 × 13-inch baking dish with nonstick cooking spray. Heat the chicken broth
in a large skillet over medium-high heat, and add the onion and garlic. Cook, stirring frequently, until the onion is tender. Transfer the onion to a mixing bowl, and
add the turkey and asparagus, tossing to combine. Layer the bread triangles in the
bottom of the baking dish, followed by the turkey mixture. Beat together the milk,
eggs, flour, mustard, salt, and pepper in a separate bowl, and pour over the turkey
and bread. Sprinkle evenly with the grated Cheddar cheese. Cover the pan with foil.
Label it, and freeze.

To Serve

Thaw the casserole in the refrigerator at least 24 hours before serving.

Preheat the oven to 350 degrees.

To serve, bake, uncovered, for about 40 minutes, or until the mixture is set and the cheese is melted and lightly browned.

Per Serving: 256.5 calories; 5.5g fat; 25.3g protein; 25.5g carbohydrates; 135mg cholesterol.

Turkey Soup

SERVES 8 TO 10

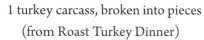

1 turkey carcass, broken into pieces
(from Roast Turkey Dinner)

4 cups fat-free chicken broth

2 whole carrots, cut into large chunks
plus 4 carrots, thinly sliced

3 medium celery stalks, cut into large
chunks

1 onion, quartered

8 cloves garlic, whole

3 bay leaves

4 carrots, sliced thinly

1 cup cooked, cubed turkey meat

2 cups frozen corn kernels

1 teaspoon thyme

3 tablespoons minced parsley

6 ounces dried macaroni

2 cups torn fresh spinach leaves

Preparation

Place the turkey carcass, chicken broth, 10 cups water, carrot chunks, celery, onion, garlic, and bay leaves into a large stockpot. Bring it to a boil, reduce the heat to low, and
cook for 1½ to 2 hours. Remove from the heat, and remove carcass and vegetables from
the broth. Put the stockpot of broth back onto the burner. Stir in the carrot slices, turkey, corn kernels, thyme, and parsley. Bring to a boil, cook 5 minutes, and remove from
the heat. Cool. Add the macaroni and spinach after the soup cools. Pour the soup into
freezer bags. Label them, and freeze.

To Serve

Thaw the soup in the refrigerator at least 24 hours before serving.

To serve, pour into a large stockpot, and heat over medium-high heat until the
soup is heated through and the noodles are tender.

Per Serving: 180 calories; 1.5g fat; 17.1g protein; 29.4g carbohydrates; 10mg
cholesterol.

Turkey-Tortilla Casserole

SERVES 6

◆▸◆◂◆

10 (6-inch) corn tortillas

Vegetable oil for frying plus
   1 tablespoon

1 large onion, chopped

2 cloves garlic, minced

1 (10-ounce) can tomatoes and
   green chiles, undrained and
   chopped

1 (7½-ounce) can whole tomatoes,
   undrained and chopped

1½ teaspoons dried cilantro

¼ teaspoon salt

2 cups cooked, cubed turkey meat

8 ounces (2 cups grated) low-fat
   Monterey Jack cheese

For Serving Day

Sour cream, if desired

Advanced Prep

Roast and cube turkey. Grate cheese. Chop onion. Mince garlic.

Preparation

Fry tortillas, one at a time, in ¼ inch hot oil for about 5 seconds on each side or until softened. Drain the tortillas on paper towels. Line an 11 × 6-inch baking dish with the tortillas, extending them above the top of the pan because they shrink during baking. Set aside.

Heat the 1 tablespoon oil in a large skillet over medium heat, and sauté the onion and garlic until tender. Stir in the tomatoes, cilantro, and salt, and cook for 5 minutes, stirring occasionally. Stir in the turkey, mixing well. Pour the turkey mixture over the tortillas. Cool. Sprinkle with grated cheese. Cover with foil. Label it, and freeze.

To Serve

Thaw the casserole in the refrigerator at least 24 hours before serving.

Preheat the oven to 350 degrees.

To serve, bake for 25 to 30 minutes. Serve with sour cream, if desired.

Per Serving: 318.1 calories; 8.7g fat; 31.8g protein; 26.5g carbohydrates; 46mg cholesterol.

12
★ ★ ★

GROUND TURKEY MINI SESSION

Turkey Loaf
Turkey Burgers

Sloppy Turkey Joes
Turkey Lasagna Roll-Ups

Ingredients List

Meat

5½ pounds lean ground turkey

Dairy

4 large eggs

1 cup fat-free cottage cheese

2 ounces reduced-fat mozzarella cheese

Parmesan cheese, grated

Bread/Pasta

Old-fashioned rolled oats

3 slices bread (to make soft bread crumbs)

12 hamburger buns

11 large lasagna noodles

Vegetables

3 medium onions

2 red bell peppers

6 cloves garlic

1 bunch green onions

4 ounces fresh mushrooms

Canned/Boxed

1 fat-free chicken broth

8 ounces tomato sauce

1 (26-ounce) jar commercial spaghetti sauce

Seasonings and Staples

Oregano

Salt

Pepper

Parsley

Italian seasoning

⅓ cup dried breadcrumbs

1 bottle chili sauce (or catsup)

Dry white wine

Nonstick cooking spray

Worcestershire sauce

Hot pepper sauce

Red wine vinegar

Preparation Instructions

Vegetable Prep

    3 medium onions: chop finely

    ¼ cup green onion: chop finely

    2 cups red bell pepper: chop

    4 ounces mushrooms: chop finely

    6 cloves garlic: mince

Cheese Prep

    2 ounces reduced-fat mozzarella cheese: grate

Misc. Prep

    3 slices day-old bread: remove crusts; crumble into crumbs.

Turkey Loaf

SERVES 6

2 pounds lean ground turkey

½ cup old-fashioned rolled oats

⅓ cup chili sauce or catsup

⅓ cup diced onion

1 egg

1 clove garlic, minced

1 teaspoon oregano

½ teaspoon salt

⅛ teaspoon pepper

Advanced Prep

Chop onion. Mince garlic.

Preparation

Preheat the oven to 350 degrees. Combine all the ingredients in a large mixing bowl, stirring well to combine. Shape the mixture into a loaf, and place into a baking dish. Bake for 40 minutes. Remove from the oven, and cool. Wrap in foil. Label it, and freeze.

To Serve

Thaw the loaf in the refrigerator at least 24 hours before serving.

Preheat the oven to 325 degrees.

To serve, bake at for 20 minutes, or until heated through. Slice and serve, reserving any leftovers for meatloaf sandwiches.

Per Serving: 233.7 calories; 12.6g fat; 22.3g protein; 6.4g carbohydrates; 91mg cholesterol.

Turkey Burgers

SERVES 6

1 egg white

¼ cup dry white wine

⅓ cup fresh breadcrumbs from day-old bread

¼ cup thinly sliced green onions

¼ teaspoon salt

⅛ teaspoon pepper

1 pound lean ground turkey

4 ounces fresh mushrooms, finely chopped

6 hamburger buns, split

Advanced Prep

Make soft breadcrumbs from 2 or 3 slices of day-old bread. Chop green onions and mushrooms.

Preparation

Beat the egg white and wine in a mixing bowl until blended. Stir in the breadcrumbs, green onions, salt, and pepper. Gently stir in the turkey and mushrooms. Shape the mixture into 6 patties, about ½-inch thick each. Wrap individually in wax paper or clear plastic wrap. Place the patties into a large freezer bag; place bag of patties and bag of hamburger buns together into a second freezer bag. Label them, and freeze together.

To Serve

Thaw the patties and buns in the refrigerator at least 24 hours before serving.

Preheat the broiler.

To serve, place the patties on a broiler pan, and broil about 6 inches from the heat source, turning once, until patties are lightly browned on both sides and the juices run clear when a knife is inserted in center, 8 to 10 minutes. Serve hot in the buns.

Per Serving: 257.9 calories; 8.6g fat; 18.1 protein; 24.2g carbohydrates; 60mg cholesterol.

Sloppy Turkey Joes

SERVES 6

———◆◈◆———

2 teaspoons fat-free chicken broth

2 cups chopped red bell peppers

1½ cups chopped onions

4 cloves garlic, minced

¼ teaspoon black pepper

1½ pounds ground turkey

½ teaspoon salt (optional)

½ cup tomato sauce

¼ cup bottled chili sauce or catsup

1 tablespoon Worcestershire sauce

¼ teaspoon hot pepper sauce, or to taste

1 tablespoon red wine vinegar

6 hamburger buns, split

Advanced Prep

Chop red bell peppers and onions. Mince garlic.

Preparation

Heat the chicken broth in a large skillet over medium heat, and cook the bell peppers, onions, garlic, and pepper until soft, about 3 minutes. Add the turkey and salt, stirring to break up the meat. Cook for 4 minutes, or until the meat is no longer pink. Stir in the tomato sauce, chili sauce, Worcestershire sauce, and hot pepper sauce. Bring the mixture to a boil. Remove from the heat, and stir in the vinegar. Cool. Pour into a freezer bag. Put the buns into a freezer bag. Place both bags into a larger freezer bag. Label them, and freeze.

To Serve

Thaw the patties and buns in the refrigerator at least 24 hours before serving.

To serve, heat the turkey mixture in a large skillet over medium heat until heated through. Warm the buns. Serve in the buns.

Per Serving: 330.0 calories; 11.7g fat; 24.9g protein; 30.6g carbohydrates; 90mg cholesterol.

Turkey Lasagna Roll-Ups

SERVES 8

11 large dried lasagna noodles, cooked and cooled

1 pound ground turkey

1 cup chopped onion

1 clove garlic, minced

1 (26-ounce) jar commercial spaghetti sauce

¼ cup dry white wine

3 tablespoons minced parsley

½ teaspoon salt

1 cup fat-free cottage cheese

2 ounces (½ cup grated) reduced-fat mozzarella cheese

2 eggs, slightly beaten

⅓ cup dry breadcrumbs

1 teaspoon Italian seasoning

¼ cup grated Parmesan cheese

Advanced Prep

Chop onion. Mince garlic. Grate cheese. Cook lasagna noodles according to package directions; drain and rinse in cold water. Store in large pan full of cold water in refrigerator until ready to use.

Preparation

Carefully cut in half crosswise to make 2 long, thin triangles from each piece of lasagna, and set aside. Lightly grease a 9 × 13 × 2-inch baking dish. Cook turkey, onion, and garlic in large skillet over medium heat until the turkey is browned, stirring to crumble meat. Add the spaghetti sauce, wine, parsley, and salt. Stir well, and cover. Reduce heat to medium-low, and cook 10 minutes, stirring occasionally. Remove from the heat, and set aside. Combine the cottage cheese and the next 4 ingredients, stirring well. Spread the mixture evenly over the lasagna pieces. Roll the pieces up jelly-roll fashion, starting at the narrow end. Place the lasagna rolls, seam side down, in the prepared baking dish. Pour the meat sauce over the rolls, and sprinkle with Parmesan cheese. Cover the pan with foil. Label it, and freeze.

To Serve

Thaw the lasagna roll ups in the refrigerator at least 24 hours before serving.

Preheat the oven to 375 degrees.

To serve, bake the roll-ups, covered, for 30 minutes. Uncover, and bake for 15 minutes more, or until heated through.

Per Serving: 462.5 calories; 13.7g fat; 24.8g protein; 58.7g carbohydrates; 80mg cholesterol.

13
★ ★ ★

Ground Beef Mini Session

Meatballs and Sauce
Beef Loaf
Pizza Burgers

Macaroni and Beef
Tortilla Casserole

Ingredients List

Meat

6 pounds extra-lean ground beef

Dairy

1 cup skim milk

12 ounces fat-free mozzarella cheese

¾ cup fat-free sour cream

Parmesan cheese, grated

2 large eggs

Butter

Bread/Pasta

1 cup dry breadcrumbs

5 slices bread, for fresh crumbs

6 ounces dried elbow macaroni

6 corn tortillas

6 hamburger buns

Vegetables

3 medium onions

1 pound carrots

1 medium-sized red bell pepper

3 medium zucchini

2 cloves garlic

½ cup sliced fresh mushrooms

1 bunch fresh cilantro

Canned/Boxed	Seasonings and Staples
1 package taco seasoning mix	Basil
1 (24-ounce) can tomato sauce	Oregano
1 (32-ounce) can crushed tomatoes	Thyme
1 (14.5-ounce) can diced tomatoes	Sage
1 (16-ounce) can red kidney beans	Parsley
1 (4.5-ounce) can chopped green chiles	Salt
	Pepper
	Apple juice or white wine

Preparation Instructions

Vegetable Prep

3 medium zucchinis: grate

3 medium onions: chop

1 medium red bell pepper: chop

1 pound carrots: shred

2 cloves garlic: mince

½ cup mushrooms: slice thinly

Cheese Prep

12 ounces fat-free mozzarella: grate

Misc. Prep

6 ounces dried elbow macaroni: cook according to package directions, drain and rinse in cold water, and store in large pan full of cold water in refrigerator until ready to use.

3 slices day-old bread: remove crust; cut or crumble into crumbs.

Meatballs and Sauce

SERVES 6

1 cup dry breadcrumbs

¾ cup skim milk

2 pounds extra-lean ground beef

1½ cups grated zucchini

¾ cup apple juice or white wine, divided

3 tablespoons grated Parmesan cheese

3 tablespoons tomato paste

1 tablespoon oregano, divided

32 ounces canned crushed tomatoes

Advanced Prep

Grate zucchini.

Preparation

Mix the breadcrumbs and milk together, and let stand for 5 minutes. Stir in the beef, zucchini, 2 tablespoons apple juice, cheese, tomato paste, and 1 teaspoon oregano. Mix well. Form into 36 uniform-sized meatballs. Spray a large skillet with nonstick cooking spray, and heat it over medium-high heat. Add the meatballs, and cook, turning as needed, until browned on all sides, about 10 minutes. Remove the meatballs from the skillet, and set aside. In the same skillet, cook the remaining apple juice over medium-high heat, scraping brown bits from bottom of skillet. Add tomatoes, remaining oregano, and 1 cup water. Reduce the heat to low. Add the meatballs, and cook, covered, for 30 to 40 minutes, or until the meatballs are cooked through. Cool. Place them into a freezer bag. Label it, and freeze.

To Serve

Thaw the meatballs in the refrigerator at least 24 hours before serving.

To serve, heat the meatballs in a skillet over medium heat until heated through.

Per Serving: 270.8 calories; 11.5g fat; 15.8g protein; 26.8g carbohydrates; 40mg cholesterol.

Beef Loaf

SERVES 8

2 cups chopped onion

2 cups shredded carrots

2 cups shredded zucchini

2 cloves garlic, minced

1 cup fresh breadcrumbs

4 tablespoons skim milk

1 pound extra-lean ground beef

2 eggs, slightly beaten

2 tablespoons minced parsley

½ teaspoon salt

2 teaspoons pepper

1 teaspoon thyme

½ teaspoon sage

Advanced Prep

Chop onions. Shred carrots and zucchini. Mince garlic. Prepare soft bread crumbs.

Preparation

Preheat the oven to 350 degrees. Spray a large skillet with nonstick cooking spray, and heat it over medium-high heat. Cook the onions until golden brown. Add the carrots, zucchini, and garlic, stirring constantly, until the vegetables are softened. Remove from the heat, and set aside to cool. Set aside. In small bowl, combine breadcrumbs and milk. Let stand 5 minutes. Combine the beef, eggs, parsley, salt, pepper, thyme, sage, vegetables, and breadcrumbs. Shape the mixture into a loaf, and place it in the center of a 9 × 13 × 2-inch baking dish. Bake for 1 hour and 15 minutes. Remove from the oven. Cool. Wrap the loaf in foil. Label it, and freeze.

To Serve

Thaw the meatloaf in the refrigerator at least 24 hours before serving.

Preheat the oven to 350 degrees.

To serve, bake the meatloaf for 30 minutes, or until heated through. Or, reheat it in a microwave.

Per Serving: 206.4 calories; 10.3g fat; 13.7g protein; 15.1g carbohydrates; 105mg cholesterol.

Pizza Burgers

SERVES 6

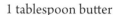

1 tablespoon butter

½ cup thinly sliced fresh mushrooms

1 pound extra-lean ground beef

1 teaspoon salt

1 teaspoon pepper

1 teaspoon oregano

½ cup tomato sauce

4 ounces (1 cup grated) fat-free
   mozzarella cheese

1 tablespoon minced parsley

6 hamburger buns, split.

Advanced Prep

Slice mushrooms. Grate cheese.

Preparation

Heat the butter in a large skillet over medium-high heat, and sauté the mushroom slices. Remove from the heat, and set aside to cool. Place the mushroom slices in a small freezer bag. Combine the beef, salt, pepper, and oregano in a mixing bowl. Form the beef mixture into six equal-sized patties. Wrap each individually in foil, and put into a freezer bag. Wrap individually; place into labeled freezer bag. Place the 2 bags into a larger freezer bag. Label it, and freeze.

To Serve

Thaw the patties in the refrigerator at least 24 hours before serving.

To serve, cook the patties in a nonstick skillet for 3 minutes, turning so both sides cook. Spread each patty with 1 tablespoon tomato sauce and 1 tablespoon mushrooms. Divide cheese evenly among the patties. Cover, and cook until the patties are cooked through and the cheese is melted. Garnish each patty with parsley, and serve in hamburger buns.

Per Serving: 217.1 calories; 13.1g fat; 21.0g protein; 3.5g carbohydrates; 56mg cholesterol.

Macaroni and Beef

SERVES 6

---

1 pound extra-lean ground beef

1 cup chopped onions

1 cup chopped red bell pepper

1 cup tomato sauce

½ teaspoon dried basil

½ teaspoon dried thyme

¼ teaspoon pepper

6 ounces dry elbow macaroni, cooked and cooled

4 ounces (1 cup grated) reduced-fat mozzarella cheese

Advanced Prep

Grate cheese. Chop onion and red bell pepper. Cook macaroni according to package directions; drain and rinse in cold water; place into large pan full of cold water in refrigerator until ready to use.

Preparation

Cook the ground beef, onion, and bell pepper in a large skillet over medium heat until the beef is no longer pink and the vegetables are softened. Add the tomato sauce, basil, thyme, and pepper. Cook, stirring frequently, until heated through. Remove from the heat. Add the macaroni, and stir to combine. Cool. Spoon into a freezer bag. Place the grated mozzarella cheese in a small freezer bag. Attach the two bags. Label them, and freeze.

To Serve

Thaw the meat and cheese in the refrigerator at least 24 hours before serving. Preheat the oven to 350 degrees.

Spoon the meat mixture into a 1-quart baking dish, and sprinkle evenly with the cheese. Bake for 20 to 30 minutes. or until bubbling and lightly browned. Serve hot.

Per Serving: 292.2 calories; 10.3g fat; 21.3g protein; 28.3g carbohydrates; 43mg cholesterol.

Tortilla Casserole

SERVES 6

1 pound extra-lean ground beef

1 (15-ounce) can red kidney beans, drained and rinsed

1 (14.5-ounce) can diced tomatoes, undrained

1 (4.5-ounce) can chopped green chiles

1 package taco seasoning mix

6 corn tortillas

¾ cup fat-free sour cream

4 ounces (1 cup grated) mozzarella or Cheddar cheese

2 tablespoons chopped fresh cilantro

Advanced Prep

Chop cilantro. Grate cheese.

Preparation

Spray a nonstick skillet with nonstick cooking spray, and heat over high heat. Add the ground beef, and cook for 8 to 10 minutes, stirring constantly, until the meat is cooked through and browned. Drain well, and add the beans, tomatoes, chiles, and taco seasoning mix; mix well. Reduce the heat to low, and cook for 5 minutes. Meanwhile, spray a 2-quart baking dish with nonstick cooking spray. Cut each tortilla in half; place the 6 halves in the bottom of the prepared dish, overlapping each slightly. Spoon half the beef mixture evenly over the tortillas. Spoon the sour cream over the beef mixture, spreading it out evenly. Top with the remaining 6 tortilla halves and beef mixture. Cover tightly with foil. Label it, and freeze.

To Serve

Thaw the casserole in the refrigerator at least 24 hours before serving.

Preheat the oven to 350 degrees.

To serve, bake for 45 minutes. Remove from the oven, and sprinkle with cheese. Cover, and let stand for 3 minutes, or until the cheese is melted. Garnish with cilantro, and serve hot.

Per Serving: 324.9 calories; 10.8g fat; 23.8g protein; 34.2g carbohydrates; 45mg cholesterol.

14
★ ★ ★

BEEF
MINI SESSION

Country Beef Soup
Old-Fashioned Beef Stew
Braised Beef

Beef Fajitas
Beef and Noodles

Ingredients List

Meat
   6 pounds lean boneless beef

Dairy
   8 ounces reduced-fat Cheddar cheese
   Margarine
   Fat-free sour cream

Bread/Pasta
   12 flour tortillas
   6 ounces wide egg noodles

Vegetables
   10 medium onions
   1 pound potatoes
   1 pound small red potatoes
   3 large stalks celery
   1 green bell pepper
   1½ cups baby carrots
   4½ cups fresh mushrooms
   1½ pounds carrots
   3 cloves garlic
   1½ cups pearl onions
   1 head lettuce

Canned/Boxed

    2 cans Italian-style stewed tomatoes

    4½ cups fat-free beef broth

    6 packets instant beef broth and
        seasoning mix

    small can tomato paste

Seasonings and Staples

    Parsley

    Salt

    Pepper

    Flour, all-purpose

    Thyme

    Tarragon

Bay leaves

Oregano

Cumin, ground

Paprika

Olive oil

Dry red wine

Lime juice

1 cup salsa (mild, medium, or hot)

Prepared mustard

Red wine vinegar

Frozen

    1 cup frozen corn kernels

Preparation Instructions

Meat Prep

    2 pounds beef: cut into 2-inch cubes

    2 pounds beef: cut into ¼-inch strips

Vegetable Prep

    5½ cups onion: chop

    3 medium onions: slice thinly

    1 green bell pepper: slice

    4 cups carrots: chop

    3 cloves garlic: mince

    1 pound small red potatoes: cut into quarters; store in large pan of water in
        refrigerator until ready to use.

    1 pound regular potatoes: peel and cut into ½-inch cubes

    1 lime: squeeze juice into small bowl

    3 cups mushrooms: remove ends

Country Beef Soup

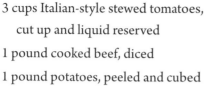

3 cups Italian-style stewed tomatoes, cut up and liquid reserved

1 pound cooked beef, diced

1 pound potatoes, peeled and cubed

1½ cups sliced celery

1½ cups sliced mushrooms

1½ cups sliced carrots

1 cup chopped onion

1 cup frozen corn kernels

6 packets instant beef broth and seasoning mix

2 tablespoons minced parsley

1 teaspoon pepper

Advanced Prep

Dice beef; sauté in large skillet until cooked through. Peel potatoes, cut into ½-inch cubes, and store in large pan of cold water in refrigerator until ready to use. Slice celery, mushrooms, and carrots. Chop onion.

Preparation

Combine all the ingredients plus 6 cups water in a large stockpot or Dutch oven. Bring to a boil, reduce the heat to medium-low, and cook until the potatoes are not quite tender. Remove from the heat, and cool quickly. Pour into freezer bags. Label them, and freeze.

To Serve

Thaw the soup in the refrigerator at least 24 hours before serving.

To serve, heat in a stockpot or Dutch oven over medium-high heat until heated through.

Per Serving: 329.0 calories; 15.5g fat; 19.3g protein; 30.9g carbohydrates; 51mg cholesterol.

Old-Fashioned Beef Stew

SERVES 6

1 tablespoon olive oil

1½ cups chopped onions

2 cloves garlic, minced

3 teaspoons flour

1 teaspoon salt, divided

½ teaspoon pepper

1 pound lean boneless beef, cut into
2-inch cubes

1 cup small white mushrooms, ends
removed

1½ cup pearl onions

1½ cup baby carrots

3 cups reduced-fat beef broth

½ cup red wine vinegar

2 tablespoons tomato paste

½ teaspoon thyme

½ teaspoon tarragon

2 bay leaves

1 pound small red potatoes, quartered

For Serving Day

2 tablespoons minced parsley

Advanced Prep

Chop onions. Mince garlic. Cut beef into 2-inch cubes. Cut small red potatoes into quarters; store in large pan of water in refrigerator until ready to use.

Preparation

Heat the oil in a large skillet over medium heat, and sauté the onions and garlic until softened. Combine the flour, half the salt, and half the pepper. Dredge the beef with the flour mixture to coat evenly. Add the beef to the onion mixture, and cook, stirring frequently, until the meat is brown on all sides. Add the mushrooms, pearl onions, and carrots; cook, stirring frequently, for 2 minutes. Add the broth, vinegar, tomato paste, thyme, tarragon, bay leaves, remaining salt and pepper, and 5 cups water. Bring to a boil, and reduce the heat to low. Cover, and cook for 20 minutes. Add the potatoes, and cook 5 minutes more; the potatoes will still be firm. Remove from the heat, and cool quickly. Pour into freezer bags. Label them, and freeze.

To Serve

Thaw the soup in the refrigerator at least 24 hours before serving.

To serve, heat over medium heat in a stockpot until heated through. Discard the bay leaves, and stir in the parsley. Serve hot.

Per Serving: 303.7 calories; 12.8g fat; 24.8g protein; 28.3g carbohydrates; 48mg cholesterol.

Braised Beef

6 SERVINGS

———◆◆◆◆———

1 tablespoon olive oil

4 cups chopped onions

4 cups chopped carrots

1 clove garlic, minced

2 pounds lean boneless beef

¼ teaspoon salt

1 cup dry red wine

1 bay leaf

1 teaspoon oregano

1 teaspoon thyme

Advanced Prep

Chop onion and carrots. Mince garlic.

Preparation

Heat the oil in a Dutch oven over medium-high heat. Add the onions, and cook, stirring often, until the onions are golden brown. Add the carrots and garlic, and cook until the carrots are tender. Add the beef to the vegetable mixture, and cook until the beef is browned. Stir in the remaining ingredients; bring to a boil. Reduce the heat to low, cover, and cook for 1½ hours, adding water as needed to prevent the meat from sticking. Remove the beef, and slice it. Cool. Place the meat and vegetable mixture into freezer bags. Label them, and freeze.

To Serve

Thaw the meat and vegetables in the refrigerator at least 24 hours before serving.

To serve, heat the mixture in a large skillet over medium heat. Serve hot.

Per Serving: 438.2 calories; 23.0g fat; 32.8g protein; 18.0g carbohydrates; 97mg cholesterol.

Beef Fajitas

SERVES 6

◆◆◆◆◆

1 pound lean boneless beef, cut into ¼-inch-thick strips

1 teaspoon ground cumin

1 teaspoon chili powder

½ teaspoon pepper

1 green bell pepper, seeded and sliced

1 cup sliced onion

¼ cup lime juice

For Serving Day

12 (6-inch) flour tortillas

2 cups shredded lettuce

8 ounces (2 cups grated) reduced-fat Cheddar cheese

1 cup salsa (mild, medium, or hot)

Advanced Prep

Slice onion and green pepper. Cut raw meat into ¼-inch slices. Store in refrigerator until ready to use.

Preparation

Season the beef all over with cumin, chili powder, and black pepper. Spray large skillet with nonstick cooking spray, and heat it over high heat. Add the bell pepper and onion, and cook, stirring constantly, until the vegetables are lightly browned. Add the beef, stirring constantly, until the beef is no longer pink. Add lime juice, and toss to combine. Cool. Put the meat and vegetables into a freezer bag. Label it, and freeze.

To Serve

Thaw the meat mixture in the refrigerator at least 24 hours before serving. Preheat the oven to 350 degrees.

To serve, reheat the meat mixture in a large skillet until heated through. Warm the tortillas in a microwave, if desired. To assemble the fajitas, place an equal amount of beef mixture onto the center of each tortilla, top the beef with

¼ cup lettuce, an equal amount of cheese, and 2 tablespoons salsa. Roll tortillas to enclose filling.

Per Serving: 386.0 calories; 7.8g fat; 31.8g protein; 47.3g carbohydrates; 41mg cholesterol.

Beef and Noodles

SERVES 6

◆─◆─◆

1 pound lean boneless beef, cut into
¼-inch-wide strips

2 medium onions, thinly sliced

2 cups small mushrooms, ends
removed

2 tablespoons margarine

2 tablespoons all-purpose flour

1 ½ cups fat-free beef broth

1 teaspoon prepared mustard

½ teaspoon paprika

½ teaspoon salt

¼ teaspoon pepper

¼ cup fat-free sour cream

For Serving Day

6 ounces dried broad egg noodles

Advanced Prep

Cut beef into ½-inch strips. Slice onions. Store in refrigerator until ready to use.

Preparation

Spray a large skillet with nonstick cooking spray, and heat it over medium-high heat. Cook the beef, stirring often, until no longer pink. Remove the beef from the skillet. In the same skillet, add the onions, cooking until golden brown. Add the mushrooms, cooking until softened and lightly browned. Remove the vegetables from the skillet. In the same skillet, heat the margarine, and sprinkle it with flour. Cook over medium-high heat until bubbling, stirring constantly, and stir in the broth, mustard, paprika, salt, and pepper. Cook, stirring constantly, until the mixture thickens. Remove from the heat. Stir in the sour cream. Return beef, onions and mushrooms to skillet, and stir gently to coat. Pour into freezer bags. Label them, and freeze.

To Serve

Thaw the meat in the refrigerator at least 24 hours before serving.

To serve, reheat the meat mixture until heated through. Cook the noodles. Serve the beef over hot noodles.

Per Serving: 322.6 calories; 11.4g fat; 25.9g protein; 32.0g carbohydrates; 76mg cholesterol.

15

PORK CHOP
MINI SESSION

Dijon Pork Chops
Sweet-n-Sour Pork
Pork-Rice Skillet Bake

Herbed Pork Chops
Provençal Pork
Stuffed Pork Chops

Ingredients List

Meat

- 18 regular pork chops
- 6 thick-cut pork chops (about 1-inch thick; ask your butcher)
- 3½ pounds boneless pork chops

Dairy

- Parmesan cheese, grated
- 1 large egg
- Butter
- Margarine

Bread/Pasta

- ½ cup unseasoned dry breadcrumbs
- 1 box wild rice mix

Vegetables

- 4 medium onions
- 1 large green bell pepper
- 3 cloves garlic
- 2 large tomatoes
- 2 cups sliced fresh mushrooms
- 1½ pounds potatoes
- 1 bunch fresh parsley

Canned/Boxed

    1 (15-ounce) can stewed tomatoes

    2 cups pineapple chunks

    1½ cups fat-free beef broth

    1 package brown and wild rice
        mushroom recipe mix

Seasonings and Staples

    Basil

    Cayenne, ground

    Parsley

    Paprika

    Mixed herbs

Fennel

Marjoram

Salt

Pepper

Cornstarch

Sugar

Vegetable oil

Dijon-style mustard

White vinegar

Catsup

Soy sauce

⅓ cup cooking sherry

⅓ cup dry white wine

Preparation

Meat Prep

    1½ pounds pork chops: trim off any fat and cut into 1-inch pieces

    2 pounds pork chops: cut into ½-inch strips

Vegetable Prep

    1 large onion: cut into thin wedges

    3 medium onions: slice thinly

    1 medium onion: chop

    1 large green pepper: cut into 1-inch squares

    1½ pounds potatoes: peel and slice thinly; store in large bowl filled with water
        in refrigerator until ready to use.

    3 cloves garlic: mince

    1 large tomato: cut into wedges

    1 large tomato: slice

    ½ cup fresh parsley: chop

    2 cups mushrooms: slice

Misc. Prep

Brown and wild rice mix: cook according to package directions, substituting ⅓ cup sherry for ⅓ cup water.

Dijon Pork Chops

SERVES 6

½ cup unseasoned dry breadcrumbs

3 tablespoons grated Parmesan cheese

3 tablespoons minced parsley

1 tablespoon vegetable oil

½ teaspoon pepper

6 pork chops

2 tablespoons Dijon mustard

Advanced Prep
None required for this recipe.

Preparation
Preheat the broiler. Combine the breadcrumbs, Parmesan cheese, parsley, oil, and pepper on a plate, mixing well. Spread both sides of the pork chops with the mustard, and press the chops into breadcrumb mixture, coating both sides. Spray the broiler pan rack with nonstick cooking spray, and arrange the chops on the rack. Broil the chops 5 to 6 inches from the heat element until cooked, about 6 minutes per side. Remove from the oven and cool. Place chops in single layer onto a cookie sheet; freeze. When they are frozen, pack them into a freezer bag. Label it, and freeze.

To Serve
Thaw the meat in the refrigerator at least 24 hours before serving.

To serve, reheat the chops in a skillet over medium heat until heated through, turning once.

Per Serving: 297.6 calories; 13.3g fat; 35.5g protein; 7.5g carbohydrates; 81mg cholesterol.

Sweet-n-Sour Pork

SERVES 6

¾ cup cornstarch, divided

⅓ cup white vinegar

⅓ cup sugar

2 tablespoons catsup

1½ tablespoons soy sauce

⅛ teaspoon cayenne

1 egg, beaten

6 boneless pork chops, trimmed and
cut into 1-inch chunks

1 large onion, cut into thin wedges

1 large green pepper, seeded and cut
into 1-inch squares

2 cloves garlic, minced

1 large tomato, cut into wedges

2 cups canned pineapple chunks,
drained

Advanced Prep

Trim pork chops and cut into 1-inch pieces. Cut onion into thin wedges. Cut green pepper into 1-inch squares. Mince garlic. Cut tomato into wedges.

Preparation

To make the sweet-and-sour sauce, combine ¼ cup cornstarch and the vinegar. Stir in 1 cup water, sugar, catsup, soy sauce, and cayenne; set aside. In a small bowl, beat egg. In a separate bowl, put the remaining cornstarch. Dip the pork chunks in egg, and then dip them into the cornstarch. Heat the oil in a large skillet over medium-high heat. Sauté the meat until golden brown on the outside and no longer pink inside. Using a slotted spoon, remove the meat, and set aside. Add the onion, green pepper, garlic, and 2 tablespoons water to pan, and sauté for 1 minute. Stir in the sweet-and-sour sauce, and cook, stirring constantly, until the sauce boils and thickens. Remove from the heat. Stir in the tomato and pineapple. Freeze the sauce and the meat chunks in separate freezer bags; attach the bags. Label them, and freeze.

To Serve

Thaw the meat and the sauce in the refrigerator at least 24 hours before serving.

To serve, heat sauce and meat in separate skillets over medium-high heat. Pour the sauce over the meat to serve.

Per Serving: 262.3 calories; 4.2g fat; 26.3g protein; 30.7g carbohydrates; 74mg cholesterol.

Pork-Rice Skillet Bake

SERVES 6

◆◈◆

6 pork chops

1 package brown and wild rice mushroom mix

1 large tomato, sliced

1 large onion, sliced

½ cup chopped fresh parsley

Advanced Prep

Slice onion and tomato. Chop fresh parsley.

Preparation

Preheat the oven to 350 degrees.

Spray a large nonstick skillet with nonstick cooking spray, and heat it over high heat. Place the meat in the skillet, and cook 2 minutes, turning after 1 minute. Remove from the heat. Remove the pork chops from the skillet; set aside. In freezer-safe casserole dish, stir together the drippings from the skillet, the wild rice mix and seasoning packet, and 2 cups water. Arrange the slices of tomato and onion in a single layer over the rice mixture. Sprinkle with the parsley. Arrange the pork chops over top, and cover. Bake for 30 minutes, or until the pork is no longer pink in center. Cool in refrigerator until room temperature. Cover with foil. Label it, and freeze.

To Serve

Thaw the meat in the refrigerator at least 24 hours before serving. Preheat the oven to 350 degrees.

To serve, bake for 20 minutes or until heated through. Serve hot.

Per Serving: 411.9 calories; 19.4g fat; 34.5g protein; 24.2g carbohydrates; 95mg cholesterol.

Herbed Pork Chops

SERVES 6

⅓ cup dry white wine

2 teaspoons crushed fennel

2 teaspoons basil

1 teaspoon marjoram

¼ teaspoon salt

1 clove garlic, minced

6 pork chops

Advanced Prep

Mince garlic.

Preparation

Combine together in a small bowl the wine, fennel, basil, marjoram, salt, and garlic, blending well. Set aside. Spray a large skillet with nonstick cooking spray. Cook pork chops over medium-high heat for 3 minutes. Turn the chops, and add the wine mixture. Reduce the heat to low, cover, and cook for 5 minutes, or until the pork is no longer pink. Remove from the heat, and cool. Place chops with wine sauce into freezer bags. Label them, and freeze.

To Serve

Thaw the bags in the refrigerator at least 24 hours before serving. To serve, reheat the chops with the wine mixture in a large skillet over medium heat, until heated through. Serve with wine sauce poured over the top of the pork chops.

Per Serving: 310.6 calories; 18.9g fat; 29.9g protein; 1.2g carbohydrates; 95mg cholesterol.

Provençal Pork

SERVES 6

———————◆◗◆◗◆———————

¼ cup butter, divided

2 pounds boneless pork chops, trimmed and cut into ½-inch-thick strips

2 medium onions, sliced

1 (15-ounce) can stewed tomatoes

½ teaspoon salt

¼ teaspoon pepper

½ teaspoon dried mixed herbs

1½ pounds potatoes, peeled and thinly sliced

1 tablespoon chopped parsley for garnish

Advanced Prep

Trim any excess fat off pork chops; slice into thin strips. Slice onions. Peel potatoes, slice them thinly, and store in large bowl filled with water in refrigerator until ready to use.

Preparation

Preheat the oven to 350 degrees.

Heat ⅛ cup butter in a large skillet over medium heat, and sauté the pork, until no longer pink. Remove the meat from the skillet, and set aside. Stir onions into the juices remaining in the pan, and cook until just tender. Add the tomatoes, salt, pepper, and mixed herbs, and bring to a boil. Reduce the heat to low, and cook about 5 minutes. In a freezer-safe casserole dish, layer the pork, sauce, and potatoes, ending with a layer of potatoes. Melt the remaining butter, and brush the top of the potatoes with it. Garnish with parsley. Cover casserole.

Bake for 1 hour. Remove from the oven, and cool. Label it, and freeze.

To Serve

Thaw the meat in the refrigerator at least 24 hours before serving. Preheat the oven to 350 degrees.

To serve, bake, uncovered, for 1 hour.

Per Serving: 323.9 calories; 15.0g fat; 26.3g protein; 20.4g carbohydrates; 74mg cholesterol.

Stuffed Pork Chops

SERVES 6

½ cup wild rice mix

⅓ cup plus 1 tablespoon sherry

2 tablespoons margarine or butter

2 cups sliced mushrooms

½ cup chopped onion

6 thick-cut pork chops

2 teaspoons pepper

1½ teaspoons paprika

1½ cups fat-free beef broth

2 tablespoons cornstarch

Advanced Prep

Chop onion. Slice mushrooms. Cook wild rice mixture according to package directions, substituting ⅓ cup sherry for ⅓ cup water in directions.

Preparation

Preheat the broiler.

Heat the butter in a large skillet over medium heat, and sauté the mushroom slices and onions until softened. Remove from the heat. Stir half the mushrooms into wild rice mixture. Slice a pocket in each chop. Spoon 2 to 3 tablespoons of the wild rice mixture into each chop, and close with a toothpick. Rub the chops with pepper and paprika. Broil chops on broiler rack 5 inches from the heat for about 7 minutes per side. Cool slightly. Remove the toothpicks. To make the sauce, stir together the broth and cornstarch. Add remaining sautéed mushrooms, and cook and stir until thickened and bubbly. Cook and stir for 2 minutes more. Stir in 1 tablespoon sherry. Place the chops and sauce in a large freezer bag. Label it, and freeze.

To Serve

Thaw the meat in the refrigerator at least 24 hours before serving. Preheat the oven to 375 degrees.

To serve, place the meat and sauce in a 9 × 13 × 2-inch casserole, and bake for 1 hour, or until heated through. Spoon sauce over chops before serving.

Per Serving: 397.8 calories; 19.3g fat; 35.6g protein; 17.5g carbohydrates; 95mg cholesterol.

16
★ ★ ★

CRAB
MINI SESSION

Crab Quesadillas
Crab Quiche
Crab-Rice Chowder

Crab Strata
Crab-Stuffed Manicotti

Ingredients List

Meat
    5 (7.5-ounce) cans crabmeat

Dairy
    3 ounces reduced-fat Monterey Jack
       cheese
    4 ounces reduced-fat Cheddar cheese
    4 ounces reduced-fat Swiss cheese
    10 large eggs or equivalent egg
       substitute
    1½ cups 2% milk or fat-free
       evaporated canned milk
    5½ cups skim milk

1½ cups fat-free cottage cheese

Margarine

Parmesan cheese, grated

Bread/Pasta
    12 flour tortillas
    8 slices bread, white or whole wheat
    6 manicotti tubes

Vegetables
    4 cloves garlic
    2 bunches green onions
    1 medium onion

1 cup sliced fresh mushrooms

2 cups broccoli florets

1 small red bell pepper

2 stalks celery

1 bunch fresh cilantro

Canned/Boxed

1 (4-ounce) can green chiles

2¼ cups fat-free chicken broth

Long-grain white rice

1 (17-ounce) can cream-style corn

Seasonings and Staples

Cilantro

Honey

Soy sauce

Salt

Pepper

Lemon peel

Dry mustard

Nutmeg, ground, or ground mace

⅛ cup sliced almonds

Thyme

Onion powder

Italian spice mix

Dry white wine

Lemon juice

Vegetable oil

Dijon-style mustard

Hot pepper sauce

Flour, all-purpose

Prepared mustard

Preparation Instructions

Cheese Prep

3 ounces reduced-fat Monterey Jack cheese: grate

4 ounces Swiss cheese: grate

4 ounces reduced-fat cheddar cheese: grate

Vegetable Prep

1 bunch green onions: slice

1 cup onion: chop

¼ cup celery: slice thinly

1 cup mushrooms: slice

2 cups broccoli florets: chop coarsely

½ cup red bell pepper: chop finely

1 bunch fresh cilantro: chop

4 cloves garlic: mince

Crab Quesadillas

SERVES 6

You can vary this recipe by seeding and dicing 2 medium tomatoes and sprinkling them on the crab mixture before adding the second tortilla.

1 (4-ounce) can green chiles

¼ cup dry white wine

1 tablespoon lemon juice

1 cup chopped fresh cilantro

¼ cup reduced-fat chicken broth

1 tablespoon honey

1 (7.5-ounce) can crabmeat, drained and flaked

3 ounces (¾ cup grated) reduced-fat Monterey Jack cheese

1 cup sliced green onions

12 flour tortillas

For Serving Day

Cold chili sauce, for serving

Advanced Prep

Grate Monterey Jack cheese. Slice green onions.

Preparation

Blend the chiles, wine, and lemon juice until smooth. Pour into a 2-quart saucepan. Bring to boil over medium heat, and continue cooking, stirring often, until reduced to 1 cup. Return the mixture to the blender. Add the cilantro, chicken broth, and honey, and blend to combine. Pour the sauce into a small freezer bag. In a mixing bowl, combine the crab, cheese, and sliced onions. Place the mixture into a freezer bag. Put the 2 bags and the tortillas into a large freezer bag. Label it, and freeze.

To Serve

Thaw the crab and the sauce mixture in the refrigerator at least 24 hours before serving. Preheat the oven to 450 degrees.

To serve, spray 2 cookie sheets with nonstick cooking spray. Place 6 tortillas in a single layer onto the cookie sheets. Divide the crab mixture evenly among the tortillas, spreading it almost to the edges. Top each tortilla with the remaining tortillas. Bake on 2 racks until tortillas are lightly browned; halfway through baking time, switch cookie sheets in the oven. Slide quesadillas onto cutting board; cut each into 6 wedges. Serve with cold chili sauce.

Per Serving: 421.7 calories; 9.1g fat; 26.2g protein; 58.2g carbohydrates; 42mg cholesterol.

Crab Quiche

SERVES 6

◆◆◆◆◆

Crust

- 1 cup rice, white or brown, cooked
- 1 egg, beaten
- 1 teaspoon soy sauce

Filling

- 4 ounces (1 cup grated) Swiss cheese
- 1 (7½-ounce) can crabmeat, drained and flaked
- 2 green onions, sliced

- 4 eggs, beaten
- 1½ cups 2% milk or fat-free evaporated milk
- ½ teaspoon salt (optional)
- ½ teaspoon grated lemon peel
- ¼ teaspoon dry mustard
- Dash ground nutmeg or ground mace
- ⅛ cup sliced almonds

Advanced Prep

Cook rice (or use leftover rice for crust). Grate Swiss cheese. Slice green onions.

Preparation

Preheat the oven to 350 degrees. Spray a 9-inch pie plate with nonstick cooking spray.

To make the crust, mix together the rice, the egg, and soy sauce. Spread evenly in the prepared pan. Bake for 10 minutes. Remove from the oven.

To make the filling, sprinkle the cheese on the pie crust. Top with the crabmeat, and sprinkle with the green onions. Mix together the eggs, milk, salt, lemon peel, mustard, and nutmeg. Pour over the crabmeat, and sprinkle the almonds on top.

Bake for 45 minutes, or until set. Remove from the oven, and let sit 10 minutes before slicing, if serving fresh, or cool and wrap the pie pan in foil. Label it, and freeze.

To Serve

Thaw the quiche in the refrigerator at least 24 hours before serving. Preheat the oven to 350 degrees.

To serve, slice and serve it cold in hot weather. Or reheat the quiche for 20 to 25 minutes, or until heated through.

Per Serving: 240.1 calories; 6.2g fat; 23.2g protein; 22.3g carbohydrates; 212mg cholesterol.

Crab-Rice Chowder

SERVES 6

—◆◆◆—

1 tablespoon vegetable oil

1 cup chopped onion

1 cup sliced fresh mushrooms

½ teaspoon thyme

2 cups coarsely chopped broccoli
   florets

½ cup diced red bell pepper

2 cups reduced-fat chicken broth

2 cups skim milk

1 (17-ounce) can cream-style corn

1 (7½-ounce) can crabmeat

3 cups cooked long-grain white rice

Salt, to taste

Pepper, to taste

Advanced Prep:

Cook rice. Chop onions, red bell pepper, and broccoli. Slice mushrooms.

Preparation

Heat the oil in a stockpot or Dutch oven over medium heat, and sauté the onions, mushrooms, and thyme. Cook, stirring often, until the vegetables are tender. Add the broccoli and bell pepper, and continue cooking, stirring often, until the broccoli begins to change to bright green and slightly soften. Remove from the heat. Stir in the broth, milk, corn, crabmeat, and rice, and season with salt and pepper. Cool. Spoon the mixture into a freezer bag. Label it, and freeze.

To Serve

Thaw the chowder in the refrigerator at least 24 hours before serving. To serve, pour the chowder into a large saucepan, and heat over medium heat, stirring often, just until heated through. Don't let the chowder boil.

Per Serving: 234.4 calories; 3.4g fat; 17.3g protein; 36.5g carbohydrates; 29mg cholesterol.

Crab Strata

SERVES 6

Note: You can bake the strata before freezing it, but let it sit in the refrigerator for at least 4 hours before baking. After baking, cool completely, label it, and freeze.

8 slices bread, crusts removed

1 (7½-ounce) can crabmeat, drained and flaked

¼ cup thinly sliced celery

1 green onion, thinly sliced

4 ounces (1 cup grated) reduced-fat Cheddar cheese

5 eggs or equivalent egg substitute

2½ cups skim milk

1 tablespoon prepared mustard

½ teaspoon salt

Advanced Prep

Cut off bread crusts. Slice celery and green onion. Grate 1 cup cheddar cheese.

Preparation

Spray a 9 × 13-inch baking pan with nonstick cooking spray. Arrange the bread in the bottom of the pan. Combine the crabmeat, celery, and onion in a mixing bowl, and spread it evenly of the bread. Sprinkle the cheese evenly over the crabmeat. Beat together the eggs, milk, mustard, and mustard. Wrap the pan in foil. Label it, and freeze.

To Serve

Thaw the strata in the refrigerator at least 24 hours before serving. Preheat the oven to 325 degrees.

To serve, uncover and bake for 1½ hours, or until knife inserted near center comes out clean. Let stand 10 minutes before serving.

Per Serving: 255.3 calories; 6.1g fat; 24.5g protein; 24.9g carbohydrates; 213mg cholesterol.

Crab-Stuffed Manicotti

SERVES 6

6 large dried manicotti tubes, cooked and cooled

1½ cups fat-free cottage cheese

4 cloves garlic, minced

1 teaspoon onion powder

1 (7½-ounce) can crabmeat, drained and flaked

1 teaspoon Italian seasoning

1 teaspoon Dijon mustard

¼ teaspoon salt

¼ teaspoon pepper

1 tablespoon margarine

1 cup skim milk

4 teaspoons flour

Dash hot pepper sauce

For Serving Day

¼ cup grated Parmesan cheese

Advanced Prep

Cook manicotti according to package directions; drain. Rinse with cold water. Let pasta sit in pan full of cold water until ready to use.

Preparation

Combine the cottage cheese, garlic, onion powder, crabmeat, Italian seasoning, mustard, salt, and pepper in a large bowl, mixing well. Heat the margarine in a saucepan over medium-low heat, and stir in the milk and flour. Continue cooking and stirring until the mixture thickens and starts to bubble. Stir 2 tablespoons of the white sauce into the crab mixture. Fill each manicotti tube with crab mixture. Place them in a 10 × 6 × 2-inch baking dish. Stir the hot pepper sauce into the remaining white sauce, and spoon over the manicotti. Wrap the dish in foil. Label it, and freeze.

To Serve

Thaw the manicotti in the refrigerator at least 24 hours before serving. Preheat the oven to 350 degrees.

To serve, bake for 25 minutes. Sprinkle with Parmesan cheese before serving.

Per Serving: 287.4 calories; 2.4g fat; 23.8g protein; 41.5g carbohydrates; 37mg cholesterol.

17
★ ★ ★

TUNA
MINI SESSION

***Crustless Tuna-Spinach
Quiche***

Tuna-Bean-Pasta Salad

Italian Chowder

Tuna-Mac

Tuna-Mex Casserole

Ingredients List

Meat

    9 cans tuna

Dairy

    4 ounces reduced-fat Monterey Jack
       cheese

    1 cup egg substitute or 3 eggs

    6 cups skim milk

    1 cup 2% milk

    ¼ cup margarine

    6 ounces reduced-fat Cheddar cheese

Bread/Pasta

    2½ cups elbow macaroni

3 cups small pasta shells

Dry bread crumbs

Vegetables

    1 red bell pepper

    2 cloves garlic

    4 green onions

    3 medium onions

    3 large carrots

    2 large tomatoes

    1 bunch celery

    1 bunch fresh parsley

Canned/Boxed

    1 can tomatoes with green chiles

    2 cans Italian-style stewed tomatoes

    2 (15-ounce) cans red kidney beans

Seasonings and Staples

    Flour, all-purpose

    Salt

    Pepper

    Hot pepper sauce

    Parsley

    Bay leaf

    Oregano

    Mixed herbs

    Olive oil

    White wine vinegar

    Lemon juice

Dijon-style mustard

Cornstarch

Dry mustard

Paprika

Basil

Marjoram

Thyme

Cayenne, ground

Nonstick cooking spray

White wine or white grape juice

Baking powder

Vegetable oil

1 box rye crackers

1 (10-ounce) package frozen spinach

3 cups frozen mixed vegetables

2 cups frozen peas and carrots

Preparation Instructions

Vegetable Prep

    1 cup frozen spinach: thaw and squeeze dry (squeeze in paper towels to
        remove last bit of moisture)

    1 medium red bell pepper: chop

    3 medium onions: chop

    1 cup carrots: grate

    4 large ribs celery: chop

    4 green onions: slice

    2 cloves garlic: mince

    ½ cup fresh parsley: chop

Cheese Prep

   4 ounces reduced-fat Monterey Jack cheese: grate.

   6 ounces reduced-fat Cheddar cheese: grate.

Misc. Prep

   3½ cups dried elbow macaroni: cook according to directions until almost
   tender; drain.

Crustless Tuna-Spinach Quiche

SERVES 6

◆◆◆◆

1 can (6 -ounce) water-packed tuna,
    drained and flaked

4 ounces (1 cup grated) reduced-fat
    Monterey Jack cheese

1 cup frozen spinach, thawed and
    squeezed dry

½ cup diced red bell pepper

½ cup chopped onion

¼ cup flour

½ teaspoon salt (optional)

1 teaspoon baking powder

1 cup egg substitute or 3 eggs

1 cup 2% milk (or 8 ounces fat-free
    evaporated milk)

½ teaspoon hot pepper sauce

Advanced Prep

Grate cheese. Chop red bell pepper and onion. Thaw frozen spinach and squeeze dry (squeeze in paper towels to remove last bits of moisture).

Preparation

Mix together the tuna, cheese, spinach, bell pepper, onion, flour, salt, and baking powder in a large bowl. Spoon the mixture into a 1-gallon freezer bag. Whisk together the egg substitute, milk, and hot pepper sauce. Pour into the freezer bag over the tuna mixture. Squeeze the air from the bag, and close. Label it, and freeze.

To Serve

Thaw the quiche in the refrigerator at least 24 hours before serving. Preheat the oven to 350 degrees. Spray a 9-inch pie plate with nonstick cooking spray.

To serve, squeeze or shake bag to recombine quiche mixture, or pour into mixing bowl and stir to combine. Pour the quiche mixture into the pie plate, spreading the filling out evenly. Bake for 40 to 50 minutes, or until a knife inserted in the center comes out clean. Important: Let stand 10 minutes before slicing or serving. Cut into 6 equal wedges.

Per Serving: 190.8 calories; 6.9g fat; 20.0g protein; 10.8g carbohydrates; 17mg cholesterol.

Tuna-Bean-Pasta Salad

SERVES 6

½ cup olive oil

3 tablespoons white wine vinegar

1 tablespoon lemon juice

1 tablespoon Dijon mustard

2 (15-ounce) cans red kidney beans, drained and rinsed

2 (7-ounce) cans tuna, drained and flaked

4 green onions, sliced

1 tablespoon dried mixed herbs

For Serving Day

3 cups small dried pasta shells

Advanced Prep

Slice green onions.

Preparation

Mix the first four ingredients together thoroughly. Stir in the kidney beans, tuna, green onions, and herbs. Spoon into a freezer bag. Squeeze the air from the bag, and close. Label it, and freeze.

To Serve

Thaw the quiche in the refrigerator at least 24 hours before serving.

To serve, squeeze the bag gently to recombine. Cook the pasta shells according to package directions until just tender. Rinse thoroughly in cold water, and drain. Put the pasta shells into a large mixing bowl. Stir in the bean-tuna mixture until well combined. Serve as a salad main course, or as a side dish.

Per Serving: 571.6 calories; 20.0g fat; 28.3g protein; 71.1g carbohydrates; 14mg cholesterol.

Italian Chowder

SERVES 6

◆❖◆

¼ cup olive oil

1 cup chopped onions

1 cup grated carrots

1 cup chopped celery

½ cup minced fresh parsley

2 cups dry white wine or white grape juice

1 bay leaf

2 cups Italian-style stewed tomatoes

2 teaspoons salt

½ teaspoon pepper

½ teaspoon dried oregano

2 cans tuna, drained

Advanced Prep

Chop onions and celery. Grate carrots.

Preparation

Heat the olive oil in a large saucepan over medium heat, and sauté the onions, carrots, celery, and parsley for 10 minutes. Stir in the wine and bay leaf. Reduce the heat to low, and cook 10 minutes more. Cool. Add the tomatoes, salt, pepper, oregano, and tuna. Pour the chowder into a freezer bag. Squeeze the air from the bag, and close. Label it, and freeze.

To Serve

Thaw the quiche in the refrigerator at least 24 hours before serving. To serve, pour into a large saucepan or Dutch oven, and add 4 cups water. Heat for 10 minutes over medium heat, or until heated through.

Per Serving: 235.9 calories; 9.7g fat; 13.6g protein; 12.3g carbohydrates; 14mg cholesterol.

Tuna-Mac

6 SERVINGS

◆—◆—◆

¼ cup margarine

1 cup chopped onion

½ cup chopped celery

2 cloves garlic, minced

2 cups dried elbow macaroni, cooked until just tender and cooled

½ cup cornstarch

1 teaspoon salt

½ teaspoon pepper

4 cups skim milk

4 ounces (1 cup grated) reduced-fat Cheddar cheese

2 cups mixed frozen peas and carrots

½ teaspoon dry mustard

2 (7-ounce) cans tuna, drained and flaked

For Serving Day

¼ cup dry breadcrumbs

1 tablespoon margarine, melted

½ teaspoon paprika

Advanced Prep

Cook macaroni according to package directions, until just tender. Chop onion and celery. Mince garlic. Grate cheese.

Preparation

Heat the margarine in a saucepan over medium heat, and sauté the onion, celery, and garlic until tender. Stir in the cornstarch, salt, and pepper. Stir in the milk, and cook, stirring often, until the mixture is thick and bubbly. Remove from the heat. Stir in the cheese, peas and carrots, dry mustard, and macaroni, until the cheese melts. Fold in the tuna. Cool in the refrigerator. Spoon into a freezer bag. Squeeze the air from the bag, and close. Label it, and freeze.

To Serve

Thaw the mixture in the refrigerator at least 24 hours before serving. Preheat the oven to 375 degrees.

To serve, pour into a 2-quart casserole, stir the breadcrumbs with the margarine and paprika, and sprinkle the mixture over top. Bake, uncovered, for 35 to 40 minutes, or until heated through.

Per Serving: 391.1 calories; 11.1g fat; 28.7g protein; 44.4g carbohydrates; 20mg cholesterol.

Tuna-Mex Casserole

SERVES 6

1½ teaspoons vegetable oil

½ cup sliced celery

½ cup chopped onions

1 (10-ounce) can tomatoes with green chiles, drained

2 cups skim milk

½ cup cornstarch

3 cups frozen mixed vegetables

2 ounces (½ cup grated) reduced-fat Cheddar cheese

½ teaspoon basil

¼ teaspoon marjoram

¼ teaspoon thyme

⅛ teaspoon ground cayenne

1½ cups dried elbow macaroni, cooked until just tender and cooled

2 (7-ounce) cans tuna, drained and flaked

For Serving Day

⅓ cup crushed rye crackers

Advanced Prep

Cook macaroni according to package directions until almost tender; drain. Slice celery. Chop onion. Grate cheese.

Preparation

Heat the oil in a saucepan over medium heat, and sauté the celery and onions until tender. Stir in the tomatoes, milk, and cornstarch. Cook over medium heat, stirring constantly, until slightly thickened. Remove from the heat. Stir in the mixed vegetables, cheese, basil, marjoram, thyme, cayenne, macaroni, and tuna. Spoon into a freezer bag. Squeeze the air from the bag, and close. Label it, and freeze.

To Serve

Thaw the dish in the refrigerator at least 24 hours before serving. Preheat the oven to 350 degrees.

To serve, pour into a 2-quart casserole. Bake for 1 hour. Sprinkle with crushed crackers for the last 10 minutes of baking. Serve hot.

Per Serving: 292.1 calories; 2.7g fat; 18.4g protein; 49.7g carbohydrates; 10mg cholesterol.

PASTA
MINI SESSION #1

Italian Pasta Bake
Linguine with Vegetables

Three-Cheese Mac-n-Cheese
Italian Garden Pasta

Ingredients List

Dairy

2½ cups skim milk

Parmesan cheese, grated

1 cup fat-free cottage cheese or fat-free ricotta

2 ounces fat-free cream cheese

2 ounces reduced-fat mozzarella cheese

6 ounces reduced-fat Cheddar cheese

Margarine

Butter

Bread/Pasta

1 pound dried pasta (any shape)

1 pound dried ziti

3 cups dried elbow macaroni

⅓ cup Italian-flavored breadcrumbs

10 ounces dried linguine

Vegetables

2 medium onions

2 medium-sized red onions

2½ pounds whole, fresh mushrooms

7 cloves garlic

Canned/Boxed

3 (16-ounce) cans Italian-style stewed tomatoes

12 ounces fat-free evaporated milk

Small can tomato paste

Seasonings and Staples

Basil

Pepper

Flour, all-purpose

Olive oil

Frozen

10 ounces frozen spinach

3 cups frozen baby carrots

3 cups frozen sugar snap peas

Preparation Instructions

Vegetable Prep

2 medium onions: chop

7 cloves garlic: mince

2 pounds mushrooms: slice

1 large red onion: slice

Cheese Prep

2 ounces reduced-fat mozzarella cheese: grate

6 ounces reduced-fat Cheddar cheese: grate

Misc. Prep

3 cups elbow macaroni: cook according to package directions, rinse in cold water, and store in refrigerator in pan full of water until ready to use.

1 pound ziti: cook according to package directions, rinse in cold water, and store in refrigerator in pan full of water until ready to use.

Frozen spinach: thaw and drain well.

Italian Pasta Bake

SERVES 6

❖◈❖

1 tablespoon olive oil

1 cup chopped onion

3 cloves garlic, minced

2 (15-ounce) cans Italian-style stewed tomatoes, puréed

1 tablespoon basil

1 pound dried ziti, cooked until just tender and cooled

1 cup fat-free cottage cheese or fat-free ricotta

¼ cup grated Parmesan cheese

2 ounces (½ cup grated) reduced-fat mozzarella cheese

Advanced Prep

Cook ziti according to package directions, but only until just tender (don't overcook). Rinse in cold water; store in refrigerator in pan full of cold water until ready to use. Chop onion. Mince garlic.

Preparation

Heat the oil in a large saucepan over medium heat, and sauté the onion and garlic until tender. Stir in the tomatoes and basil, and cook for 2 minutes. Remove from the heat. Put the ziti, cottage cheese, and Parmesan cheese into a large mixing bowl. Add the tomato–onion mixture, stirring to combine. Spoon into freezer bags. Put grated mozzarella cheese into a small freezer bag and attach it to the pasta mixture. Label them, and freeze.

To Serve

Thaw the dish in the refrigerator at least 24 hours before serving. Preheat the oven to 350 degrees.

To serve, pour into a large casserole dish, and sprinkle with the mozzarella cheese. Bake for 30 minutes, or until heated through.

Per Serving: 465.9 calories; 5.9g fat; 23.0g protein; 83.8g carbohydrates; 6mg cholesterol.

Linguine with Vegetables

SERVES 6

2 teaspoons olive oil

4 cloves garlic, minced

2 tablespoons butter

1½ cups sliced mushrooms

1½ cups sliced red onion

1½ cups fat-free evaporated milk

1 tablespoon tomato paste

3 cups frozen whole baby carrots

3 cups frozen sugar snap peas

For Serving Day

10 ounces dried linguine

¼ cup grated Parmesan cheese

Advanced Prep

Mince garlic. Slice mushrooms and red onion.

Preparation

Heat the oil in a large skillet over high heat, and sauté the garlic until golden, for 30 seconds to 1 minute. Using a slotted spoon, remove and discard the garlic. Heat the butter in the same skillet, and sauté the mushrooms and onions until crisp-tender. Stir the milk and tomato paste together in a large mixing bowl, and stir in the mushroom–onion mixture, carrots, and sugar snap peas. Spoon into freezer bags. Squeeze the air from the bag, and close. Label it, and freeze.

To Serve

Thaw the dish in the refrigerator at least 24 hours before serving.

To serve, cook the linguine according to package directions. While the pasta is cooking, heat the sauce in a skillet over medium heat, stirring often to combine, until heated through. Serve over hot linguine, and garnish with Parmesan cheese.

Per Serving: 545.4 calories; 16.0g fat; 28.7g protein; 72.8g carbohydrates; 35mg cholesterol.

Three-Cheese Mac-n-Cheese

SERVES 6

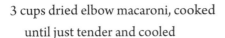

3 cups dried elbow macaroni, cooked until just tender and cooled

¼ cup flour

⅛ teaspoon pepper

2½ cups skim milk, divided

¼ cup grated Parmesan cheese

6 ounces (1½ cups grated) reduced-fat Cheddar cheese

2 ounces fat-free cream cheese, cubed

⅓ cup Italian-flavored breadcrumbs

1 tablespoon margarine, melted

Advanced Prep

Prepare macaroni according to package directions, rinse it in cold water, and store in refrigerator in pan full of cold water until ready to use. Grate cheddar cheese.

Preparation

Combine the flour and pepper in a large saucepan. Add ½ cup milk, and whisk until smooth. Gradually add the remaining milk, stirring briskly. Cook over medium heat until the mixture just barely begins to boil. Remove from the heat, and add the cheeses, stirring until melted. Stir in the macaroni. Spoon the mixture into a 9-inch-square baking dish. Mix the breadcrumbs with the margarine, and sprinkle over top. Wrap the dish in foil. Label it, and freeze.

To Serve

Thaw the dish in the refrigerator at least 24 hours before serving. Preheat the oven to 350 degrees.

To serve, bake, uncovered, for 30 minutes, or until golden brown and bubbly.

Per Serving: 294.4 calories; 5.9g fat; 22.8g protein; 36.6g carbohydrates; 15mg cholesterol.

Italian Garden Pasta

SERVES 6

3 tablespoons olive oil

1 pound mushrooms, sliced

1 medium onion, chopped

1 (16-ounce) can Italian-style stewed tomatoes, undrained and chopped

10 ounces frozen spinach, thawed and well drained

For Serving Day

1 pound dried macaroni or other favorite pasta shape

¼ cup grated Parmesan cheese

Advanced Prep

Slice mushrooms. Chop onion. Thaw spinach. Drain well. Pat with dry paper towels to remove as much liquid as possible.

Preparation

Heat the olive oil in a large saucepan, and sauté the mushrooms and onions until soft. Remove from the heat. Stir in the stewed tomatoes and juice. Stir in the spinach. Spoon into freezer bags. Label them, and freeze.

To Serve

Thaw the dish in the refrigerator at least 24 hours before serving. To serve, cook the pasta according to package directions. Heat the sauce in a large skillet over medium heat just until heated through. Toss the pasta with the sauce, and sprinkle with Parmesan cheese.

Per Serving: 405.7 calories; 9.5g fat; 14.7g protein; 66.8g carbohydrates; 3mg cholesterol.

PASTA
MINI SESSION #2

Spinach-Ricotta Bows
Spaghetti Pie
Pasta with Vegetable-Cheese Sauce

Cheese Manicotti
Florentine Shells
Creamy Penne

Ingredients List

Dairy

3 cups part-skim ricotta cheese

3½ cups fat-free cottage cheese

6 ounces (1½ cups) reduced-fat Cheddar cheese

1½ cups grated Parmesan cheese

3 tablespoons margarine

4 large eggs

12 ounces reduced-fat mozzarella cheese

Bread/Pasta

1 pound dried bow tie pasta

6 ounces dried spaghetti

1 pound dried spinach fettuccine

12 dried manicotti

18 large dried macaroni shells

10 ounces dried penne or rigatoni

Vegetables

3½ medium onions

2 green onions

9 cloves garlic

1½ cups carrots

7 cups broccoli florets

12 sun-dried tomato halves (not
  packed in oil)

3 cups cauliflower florets

Canned/Boxed

2 (16-ounce) cans Italian-style
  stewed tomatoes

1 (8-ounce) can tomato sauce

1 (6-ounce) can tomato paste

4 cups spaghetti sauce

16 ounces fat-free evaporated milk

Seasonings and Staples
  Basil

Oregano

Garlic powder

Thyme

Salt

Pepper

Nutmeg, ground

Bay leaf

Parsley

Sugar

Flour, all-purpose

Olive oil

Vegetable oil

Frozen
  3 (10-ounce) packages frozen spinach

Preparation Instructions

Vegetable Prep

2 (10-ounce) packages frozen spinach: thaw and drain, and pat dry with paper
  towels to remove as much liquid as possible.

1 large onion: chop

1 large onion: slice thinly

2 green onions: slice thinly

1½ cups carrots: slice thinly

7 cups broccoli florets: cut into large chunks

3 cups cauliflower florets: cut into large chunks

9 cloves garlic: mince

12 sun-dried tomato halves: slice

Cheese Prep

    12 ounces reduced-fat mozzarella cheese: grate

    4 ounces reduced-fat Cheddar cheese: grate

Misc. Prep

    6 ounces dried spaghetti: cook according to package directions until just tender, drain and rinse in cold water, and store in large pan full of water in refrigerator until ready to use.

    12 manicotti tubes: cook according to package directions, rinse in cold water, and store in large pan full of cold water until ready to use.

    18 large shells: cook shells according to package directions, drain and rinse in cold water, and store in large pan full of cold water in refrigerator until ready to use.

Spinach-Ricotta Bows

6 SERVINGS

2 tablespoons olive oil

1 medium onion, chopped

4 cloves garlic, minced

10 ounces frozen spinach, thawed, well drained, and squeezed dry

1½ cups part-skim ricotta or fat-free small curd cottage cheese

½ teaspoon salt

¼ teaspoon pepper

Dash ground nutmeg

For Serving Day

1 pound dried bow tie pasta

¼ cup grated Parmesan cheese

Advanced Prep

Thaw and drain spinach. Pat dry with paper towels to remove as much liquid as possible. Chop onion. Mince garlic.

Preparation

Heat the oil in a large skillet, and sauté the onions and garlic until the onion is soft. Add ½ cup water, and bring to a boil. Remove from the heat, stir in the spinach, ricotta, salt, pepper, and nutmeg. Spoon into a freezer bag. Label it, and freeze.

To Serve

Thaw the mixture in the refrigerator at least 24 hours before serving. To serve, cook the pasta according to package directions. Heat the sauce in a large skillet over medium heat just until heated through.

Spoon the sauce over the pasta, toss gently, and sprinkle with Parmesan cheese.

Per Serving: 404.6 calories; 6.9g fat; 21.9g protein; 63.8g carbohydrates; 13mg cholesterol.

Spaghetti Pie

SERVES 6

◆◀◆◀

6 ounces dried spaghetti, cooked and
cooled

2 tablespoons margarine

½ cup grated Parmesan cheese

2 eggs, well beaten

1 teaspoon vegetable oil

½ cup chopped onion

1 (16-ounce) can Italian-style stewed
tomatoes, undrained

1 (6-ounce) can tomato paste

1 teaspoon sugar

1 teaspoon oregano

½ clove garlic, minced

1 cup fat-free cottage cheese

4 ounces reduced-fat Cheddar,
mozzarella, or Monterey Jack
cheese, grated

Advanced Prep

Chop onion. Mince garlic. Cook spaghetti according to package directions. Drain. Stir margarine into hot spaghetti until melted. Stir in the Parmesan cheese and eggs. Spray a 9-inch pie plate with cooking spray. Form pasta mixture into a crust in bottom and up sides of pie plate. Cover, and store in refrigerator until ready to use.

Preparation

Heat the vegetable oil in a skillet over medium heat, and sauté the onion until soft. Add the tomatoes, tomato paste, sugar, oregano, and garlic, and heat through. Spread the cottage cheese over spaghetti crust. Top with the tomato mixture, and sprinkle with the grated cheese. Wrap the pie in foil. Label it, and freeze.

To Serve

Thaw the mixture in the refrigerator at least 24 hours before serving. Preheat the oven to 350 degrees.

To serve, bake, covered, for 25 minutes. Remove the foil, and bake for 5 minutes more, or until the cheese is lightly browned.

Per Serving: 281.9 calories; 9.0g fat; 18.1g protein; 33.3g carbohydrates; 80mg cholesterol.

Pasta with Vegetable-Cheese Sauce

SERVES 6

2 teaspoons olive oil

1½ cups thinly sliced onions

1½ cups thinly sliced carrots

3 cloves garlic, minced

1 tablespoon flour

3 cups broccoli florets

3 cups cauliflower florets

1½ cups fat-free ricotta

12 sun-dried tomato halves, sliced
(not packed in oil)

For Serving Day

1 pound dried spinach fettuccine

Advanced Prep

Slice onion and carrot. Mince garlic. Cut up broccoli and cauliflower into large chunks. Slice sun-dried tomatoes.

Preparation

Heat the oil in a skillet over medium heat, and sauté the onions, carrots, and garlic, stirring often, until the onions and carrots are soft. Sprinkle with the flour, stir, and cook for 1 minute. Add 3 cups water, and the broccoli and cauliflower. Reduce the heat to low, cover, and cook until the broccoli and cauliflower are just becoming tender. Stir in the cheese and tomatoes. Cook for 1 minute. Remove from the heat. Cool. Spoon into a freezer bag. Label it, and freeze.

To Serve

Thaw the mixture in the refrigerator at least 24 hours before serving.

To serve, cook the pasta according to package directions. Heat the sauce in a large skillet over low heat just until heated through. Spoon the sauce over the hot pasta.

Per Serving: 309.3 calories; 2.7g fat; 18.9g protein; 53.3g carbohydrates; 10mg cholesterol.

Cheese Manicotti

6 SERVINGS

1 tablespoon vegetable oil

½ cup chopped onion

1 clove garlic, minced

1 (16-ounce) can Italian-style stewed
tomatoes, cut up

1 (8-ounce) can tomato sauce

1 teaspoon sugar

1 teaspoon oregano

1 teaspoon thyme

¼ teaspoon salt

1 bay leaf

2 eggs, beaten

1½ cups fat-free cottage cheese

8 ounces (2 cups grated) reduced-fat
mozzarella cheese

¼ cup grated Parmesan cheese

¼ cup minced parsley

Dash pepper

12 manicotti, cooked until just
tender and cooled

Advanced Prep

Chop onion. Mince garlic. Grate mozzarella cheese. Cook manicotti shells according to package directions. Rinse in cold water. Store in large pan of cold water until ready to use.

Preparation

Heat the oil in a large saucepan over medium heat, and sauté the onion and garlic until the onion is soft. Stir in the tomatoes, tomato sauce, ⅓ cup water, sugar, oregano, thyme, salt, and bay leaf. Bring to a boil, and cook, uncovered, for 45 minutes. Mix together the eggs, cottage cheese, mozzarella cheese, Parmesan cheese, parsley, and pepper. Spoon the cheese mixture into the manicotti. Pour half of tomato mixture into a 9 × 13-inch baking pan, and place the stuffed shells into the pan. Pour the remaining sauce over top. Wrap with foil. Label it, and freeze.

To Serve

Thaw the manicotti in the refrigerator at least 24 hours before serving.

Preheat the oven to 350 degrees.

To serve, bake, covered, for 45 minutes, or until hot and bubbly.

Per Serving: 410.5 calories; 7.1g fat; 32.9g protein; 54.1g carbohydrates; 86mg cholesterol.

Florentine Shells

SERVES 6

◆◀◆▶◆

1 (10-ounce) package frozen
    spinach, thawed, drained, and
    squeezed dry

4 ounces (1 cup grated) reduced-fat
    mozzarella cheese

1 cup fat-free cottage cheese

¼ cup grated Parmesan cheese

2 green onions, thinly sliced

1 tablespoon minced parsley

1 teaspoon basil

¼ teaspoon salt

¼ teaspoon ground nutmeg

¼ teaspoon pepper

18 large shells

4 cups spaghetti sauce, homemade or
    commercially prepared

Advanced Prep

Grate mozzarella cheese. Slice green onions. Cook macaroni shells according to package directions. Drain, rinse in cold water. Store in large pan of cold water until ready to use.

Preparation

Mix together the spinach, mozzarella cheese, cottage cheese, Parmesan cheese, green onions, parsley, basil, salt, nutmeg and pepper. Spray a 9 × 13-inch baking pan with nonstick cooking spray. Fill each shell with ¼ cup spinach–cheese mixture. Place the filled shells in the baking dish. Pour the spaghetti sauce evenly over the shells. Wrap with foil. Label it, and freeze.

To Serve

Thaw the shells in the refrigerator at least 24 hours before serving. Preheat the oven to 350 degrees.

To serve, bake the shells for 35 minutes, or until hot and bubbly. Let sit for 10 minutes before serving.

Per Serving: 486.2 calories; 10.1g fat; 25.0g protein; 76.6g carbohydrates; 8mg cholesterol.

Creamy Penne

SERVES 6

4 cups broccoli florets, cut into bite-sized pieces

1 tablespoon margarine

2 cups fat-free evaporated milk

2 tablespoons flour

3 teaspoons garlic powder

4 ounces (1 cup grated) reduced-fat Cheddar cheese

¼ cup grated Parmesan cheese

¼ teaspoon salt

½ teaspoon pepper

For Serving Day

10 ounces dried penne pasta

Advanced Prep

Cut broccoli into bite-sized chunks. Grate cheese. Mince garlic.

Preparation

Steam the broccoli until just tender. Drain, and rinse in cold water. Heat the margarine in a large skillet over medium heat, and stir in the milk and flour, whisking constantly until the mixture thickens. Stir in the garlic powder. Reduce the heat to low. Add the cheeses, salt, and pepper. Stir constantly, until the Cheddar cheese melts. Remove from the heat, and stir in the broccoli. Cool. Spoon into a freezer bag. Label it, and freeze.

To Serve

Thaw the mixture in the refrigerator at least 24 hours before serving.

To serve, cook the pasta according to package directions. Heat the sauce in a large skillet over low heat just until heated through. Stir the pasta gently into the sauce, and serve.

Per Serving: 320.9 calories; 4.0g fat; 20.3g protein; 51.1 carbohydrates; 8mg cholesterol.

TOFU MINI SESSION #1

Broccoli-Tofu Quiche
Tofu Fried Rice

Tofu Burgers/Loaves/Balls
Enchilada Casserole

Ingredients List

Dairy

4 ounces Monterey Jack cheese

Bread/Pasta

12 corn tortillas

Oats, old-fashioned rolled

Wheat germ

Long-grain rice

Vegetables

1 green bell pepper

3 cups broccoli

3 large onions

2 green onions

4 pounds tofu

3 cloves garlic

2 celery stalks

Canned/Boxed

½ cup sliced black olives

Seasonings and Staples

Basil

Catsup

Chili powder

Cumin, ground

Flour, all-purpose

Garlic powder

Mustard, dry	Salt
Onion powder	Lemon juice
Oregano	Soy sauce
Parsley	Vegetable oil
Pepper	

Preparation Instructions

Tofu Prep

1 pound tofu: drain and crumble. Squeeze excess water from tofu or place in colander inside larger bowl in refrigerator overnight to drain. After drained, crumble into small pieces.

1 pound tofu: mash

½ pound tofu: cut into ½-inch cubes

Vegetable Prep

3 medium onions: chop

1 green pepper: chop

2 celery stalks: slice

2 green onions: slice

3 cups broccoli: cut into bite-sized pieces. Steam broccoli until tender.

3 cloves garlic: mince

Cheese Prep

Reduced-fat Monterey Jack cheese: grate

Misc. Prep

Rice: prepare 3 cups of regular (not instant) rice.

12 corn tortillas: slice into 1-inch slices.

Broccoli-Tofu Quiche

SERVES 6

Note: You can substitute other cooked vegetables for the broccoli, and prepare the dish as usual.

3 cups cut-up broccoli	2 tablespoons lemon juice
2 tablespoons vegetable oil	1 tablespoon dry mustard
1 cup chopped onion	1 teaspoon salt
3 cloves garlic, minced	¼ teaspoon pepper
1 (1-pound) block tofu, cut in half	1 tablespoon flour

Advanced Prep

Cut up broccoli. Steam broccoli until tender. Set aside. Chop onion. Mince garlic.

Preparation

Preheat the oven to 350 degrees. Spray a 9-inch pie plate with nonstick cooking spray.

Steam the broccoli until just tender. Drain, and rinse in cold water. Heat the oil in a large skillet over medium heat, and sauté the onion and garlic until the onion is soft. Crumble half of the tofu, and set aside. Put the remainder in a blender or food processor. Add the lemon juice, mustard, salt, pepper, and flour, and process until smooth. Pour into the skillet, stirring to combine with the onion and garlic. Fold in the crumbled tofu and broccoli. Pour the mixture into the prepared pie plate. Bake for 30 minutes. Remove from the oven. Cool. Wrap with foil. Label it, and freeze.

To Serve

Thaw the quiche in the refrigerator at least 24 hours before serving.

Preheat the oven to 350 degrees.

To serve, uncover and bake for 15 to 20 minutes, or until heated through.

Per Serving: 132.0 calories; 8.6g fat; 8.2g protein; 8.1g carbohydrates; 0mg cholesterol.

Tofu Fried Rice

SERVES 6

3 tablespoons vegetable oil

2 tablespoons soy sauce

½ pound tofu, cut into ½-inch cubes

1 large onion, chopped

1 green pepper, chopped

2 celery stalks, sliced

3 cups cooked rice

2 green onions, sliced

Advanced Prep

Cook rice according to package directions. Chop onion and green pepper. Slice celery and green onions. Cut tofu into ½-inch cubes.

Preparation

Heat the oil in a skillet over high heat, add 1 tablespoon soy sauce and the tofu, and stir-fry for 1 minute. Using a slotted spoon, remove the tofu from the skillet. Stir in the onion, green pepper, and celery, and stir-fry for 3 minutes, or until the vegetables are soft. Stir in the cooked rice, 1 tablespoon soy sauce, and the tofu cubes, and stir-fry until the rice is golden. Stir in the green onion. Remove from the heat. Cool. Spoon the mixture into a freezer bag. Label it, and freeze.

To Serve

Thaw the rice in the refrigerator at least 24 hours before serving.

To serve, heat 1 tablespoon vegetable oil in a large skillet over medium-high heat. Add the rice mixture, and stir-fry until heated through.

Per Serving: 223.0 calories; 6.8g fat; 7.3g protein; 34.3g carbohydrates; 0mg cholesterol.

Tofu Burgers/Loaves/Balls

1 (1-pound) block tofu, well drained
    and mashed

½ cup old-fashioned rolled oats

½ cup wheat germ

2 tablespoons onion powder

1 tablespoon chopped parsley

1 teaspoon salt

½ teaspoon basil

½ teaspoon oregano

½ teaspoon garlic powder

For Serving Day

2 tablespoons vegetable oil

Hamburger buns for serving

Advanced Prep
Mash tofu.

Preparation
Spray cookie sheet with cooking spray. Combine the first 9 ingredients in a mixing bowl, and shape them into 8 patties. Arrange the patties in a single layer on a cookie sheet. Freeze the patties until solid, then wrap them individually, and put them into a large freezer bag. Label it, and freeze.

To Serve
Thaw the patties in the refrigerator on a cookie sheet at least 24 hours before serving. To serve, heat the vegetable oil in a large skillet, and cook the patties, turning once, until golden. Serve on buns with hamburger fixings.

Other recipe options include:

Tofu "Meatballs": Shape into 20 balls and brown in a large skillet in ½ cup hot oil.

Tofu "Meatloaf": Spray a loaf pan with cooking oil, press the mixture into the pan, and bake at 350 degrees for 30 minutes. Spread catsup over top of loaf during last 10 minutes of baking. Let sit for 10 minutes before slicing.

Per Serving: 167.7 calories; 9.6g fat; 9.8g protein; 13.1g carbohydrates; 0mg cholesterol.

Enchilada Casserole

SERVES 6

◆◀◆▶◆

2 tablespoons vegetable oil

1 cup chopped onion

3 tablespoons chili powder

3 tablespoons flour

½ teaspoon garlic powder

½ teaspoon ground cumin

1 teaspoon salt

12 corn tortillas, sliced into 1-inch-wide strips

1 (1-pound) block tofu, well drained and crumbled

4 ounces (1 cup grated) reduced-fat Monterey Jack cheese

½ cup sliced black olives

Advanced Prep

Squeeze excess water from tofu or place in colander inside larger bowl in refrigerator overnight to drain. After drained, crumble into small pieces. Chop onions. Slice tortillas into 1-inch slices.

Preparation

Heat the oil in a large skillet over medium heat, and sauté the onion until soft. Remove from the heat. Mix together the chili powder, flour, garlic powder, cumin, and salt in a large bowl. Stir the flour mixture into skillet. Gradually add 4 cups water, stirring constantly to form a smooth gravy. Return to the heat, and over medium heat, bring the mixture to a boil, stirring often. Remove from the heat, and pour half the mixture into a 9 × 9-inch-square baking dish. Layer half the tortilla strips over the gravy. Sprinkle the tofu crumbles over the tortillas, and layer on the remaining tortilla strips. Pour the remaining gravy over top. Sprinkle with the Monterey Jack cheese and black olives. Wrap the pan with foil. Label it, and freeze.

To Serve

Thaw the casserole in the refrigerator at least 24 hours before serving.

Preheat the oven to 350 degrees.

To serve, bake, uncovered, for 20 minutes, or until hot and bubbly.

Per Serving: 307.9 calories; 13.5g fat; 15.8g protein; 33.7g carbohydrates; 7mg cholesterol.

21
★ ★ ★

TOFU MINI SESSION #2

Tofu-and-Spinach Lasagna
Tamale Pie

Stuffed Shells
Tofu Sloppy Joes

Ingredients List

Dairy

    4 ounces mozzarella cheese

    2 large eggs

    2 cups skim milk

Bread/Pasta

    12 jumbo shells

    1 (1-pound) package lasagna noodles

Vegetables

    4 pounds tofu

    2 bunches fresh spinach

    3 large onions

    5 cloves garlic

    3 large green bell peppers

    1 bunch parsley

Canned/Boxed

    5 cups prepared spaghetti sauce

    1 (16-ounce) can diced tomatoes

    2 (15-ounce) can tomato sauce

    1 (8-ounce) can tomato paste

    1 (6-ounce) can chopped green chiles

    ½ cup sliced black olives

Seasonings and Staples

    Baking powder

Baking soda

Basil

Chili powder

Cornmeal

Cumin, ground

Flour, all-purpose

Garlic powder

Onion powder

Oregano

Sage

Salt

Sugar

Bay leaves

Olive oil

Soy sauce

Vegetable oil

Frozen

1 (10-ounce) package frozen corn kernels

Preparation Instructions

Tofu Prep

1 pound tofu: drain slightly (don't squeeze out excess water), place in blender or food processor, and blend until smooth. Spoon into mixing bowl; add spinach, oregano, and basil, and mix well. Store in refrigerator until ready to use.

1 pound tofu: drain well and cut into ½-inch cubes

1 pound tofu: drain and mash with potato masher.

1 pound tofu: drain well and crumble into small pieces.

Vegetable Prep

2 bunches fresh spinach (or 1 10-ounce package frozen, thawed and well drained): rinse fresh spinach in cold water, cut off thick stems, keep water clinging to leaves, and place in large stockpot. Heat, covered, over high heat; stir frequently until spinach is soft, and drain and squeeze out excess liquid.

2 medium-sized green bell peppers: chop

3 medium onions: chop

5 cloves garlic: mince

¼ cup fresh parsley: chop

Cheese Prep

4 ounces reduced-fat mozzarella cheese: grate

Misc. Prep

    12 jumbo shells: cook shells according to package direction until just soft, drain and rinse gently in cold water, and store in large pan full of cold water in refrigerator until ready to use.

Tofu-and-Spinach Lasagna

SERVES 8

Sauce

½ cup chopped onion

¼ cup chopped green bell pepper

3 cloves garlic, minced

2 bay leaves, crumbled

1 teaspoon basil

1 (16-ounce) can tomato sauce

1 (8-ounce) can tomato paste

Filling

1 pound tofu

2 bunches fresh spinach or 1
   (10-ounce) package frozen spinach

1 teaspoon oregano

Pinch sage

½ teaspoon basil

1 (1-pound) package lasagna
   noodles, uncooked

Advanced Prep

Chop green pepper and onion. Mince garlic. Rinse fresh spinach in cold water. Cut off thick stems. Keep the water clinging to the leaves. Place in large stockpot. Heat covered over high heat, stirring frequently until spinach is soft. Drain spinach and squeeze out excess liquid. Set aside. Drain tofu slightly (don't squeeze out excess water). Place in blender container or food processor. Blend until smooth, stopping to scrape sides of container frequently. Spoon blended tofu into mixing bowl. Add spinach, oregano, sage, and basil. Mix well. Store tofu and spinach in separate covered bowls in refrigerator until ready to use.

Preparation

To make the sauce, combine ¼ cup water, onion, green pepper, and garlic in a large saucepan. Bring to a boil over medium heat, and reduce the heat to medium-low, and cooking and stirring often until the vegetables are soft. Stir in the bay leaves, basil, tomato sauce, tomato paste, and 2 cups water. Cook for 15 minutes, and remove from the heat.

To assemble, spread 1 cup sauce over the bottom of a 9 × 13-inch baking pan. Layer one-third of the lasagna on the sauce, and pour another 1 cup sauce over top.

Spoon the tofu mixture by dollops over the sauce, and add a second layer of noodles, and another 1 cup sauce. Spoon in the remaining tofu mixture. Add a third layer of lasagna, pressing down firmly. Spoon the remaining sauce over the noodles, making sure that the noodles are completely covered with sauce. Wrap the pan in foil. Label it, and freeze.

To Serve

Thaw the lasagna in the refrigerator at least 24 hours before serving. Preheat the oven to 350 degrees.

To serve, bake, covered, for 40 minutes. Uncover, and continue baking 15 more minutes. Let stand 10 minutes before serving. Cut into squares to serve.

Tamale Pie

6 SERVINGS

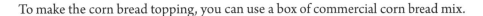

To make the corn bread topping, you can use a box of commercial corn bread mix.

2 tablespoons vegetable oil

1 cup chopped green bell pepper

1 cup chopped onion

2 cloves garlic, minced

1 pound tofu, well drained and cut
   into ½-inch cubes

2 tablespoons chili powder

½ teaspoon cumin

½ teaspoon salt

½ teaspoon oregano

1 (16-ounce) can diced tomatoes

1 (15-ounce) can tomato sauce

1 (10-ounce) package frozen corn
   kernels

1 (6-ounce) can chopped green chiles

½ cup sliced black olives

For Corn bread Topping

2 cups cornmeal

½ cup flour

1 teaspoon salt

½ teaspoon baking soda

½ teaspoon baking powder

1 tablespoon sugar

2 eggs, beaten

1 tablespoon vegetable oil

2 cups skim milk

Advanced Prep

Squeeze excess water from tofu or place in colander inside larger bowl in refrigerator overnight to drain. After drained, cut into ½-inch cubes. Chop green pepper and onion. Mince garlic.

Preparation

Spray a 9 × 13-inch baking dish with nonstick cooking spray. Heat the vegetable oil in a large skillet, and sauté the green pepper, onion, and garlic until almost soft. Stir in the tofu, chili powder, cumin, salt, and oregano, and sauté for 2 minutes. Remove from the heat. Stir in the tomatoes, tomato sauce, corn, green chiles, and black olives, and pour the mixture into dish.

Mix together the cornmeal, flour, salt, baking soda, and baking powder in a bowl. In a separate mixing bowl, stir together the sugar, eggs, oil, and milk. Gradually stir the cornmeal mixture into the milk mixture. Stir until smooth, but don't overmix. Pour cornmeal batter over the tofu mixture in the dish. Wrap with foil. Label it, and freeze.

To Serve

Thaw the dish in the refrigerator at least 24 hours before serving. Preheat the oven to 350 degrees.

To serve, bake, uncovered, for 30 minutes, or until the corn bread topping is cooked and browned.

Per Serving: 502.7 calories; 15.2g fat; 20,1g protein; 76.0g carbohydrates; 73mg cholesterol.

Stuffed Shells

SERVES 6

12 jumbo shells

1 (1-pound) block tofu, mashed

4 ounces (1 cup grated) reduced-fat
mozzarella cheese

¼ cup chopped fresh parsley

2 tablespoons onion powder

1½ teaspoon salt

½ teaspoon garlic powder

½ teaspoon basil

3 cups spaghetti sauce, homemade or
commercially prepared

Advanced Prep

Grate cheese. Mash tofu. Cook macaroni shells according to package directions. Rinse in cold water. Place in large pan of cold water until ready to use.

Preparation

Mix together the tofu, cheese, parsley, onion powder, salt, garlic powder, and basil in a large bowl. Spread 1½ cups spaghetti sauce over the bottom of a 9 × 9-inch baking pan. Fill each shell with ¼ cup tofu mixture, and place them in the pan. Stir ½ cup water into the remaining sauce, and pour over the shells. Wrap with foil. Label it, and freeze.

To Serve

Thaw the shells in the refrigerator at least 24 hours before serving. Preheat the oven to 350 degrees.

To serve, bake, uncovered, for 30 minutes, or until bubbly.

Per Serving: 441.5 calories; 10.5g fat; 22.1g protein; 66.7g carbohydrates; 3mg cholesterol.

Tofu Sloppy Joes

SERVES 6

2 tablespoons oil

1 cup chopped onion

1 cup chopped green pepper

1 (1-pound) block tofu, crumbled

2 tablespoons soy sauce

2 cups spaghetti sauce, homemade or commercially prepared

1 tablespoon chili powder

6 hamburger buns

Advanced Prep

Chop onion and green pepper. Crumble tofu.

Preparation

Heat the vegetable oil in a large skillet over medium heat, and sauté the onion and green pepper until soft. Mix together the tofu and soy sauce in a bowl, and add to the onion and green pepper. Continue sautéing until the tofu begins to brown. Remove from the heat. Stir in the spaghetti sauce and chili powder. Spoon into freezer bags. Label them, and freeze.

To Serve

Thaw the sloppy joe mixture in the refrigerator at least 24 hours before serving.

To serve, heat the mixture in large skillet over medium heat until heated through. Serve on hamburger buns.

Per Serving: 209.9 calories; 12.4g fat; 8.6g protein; 19.2g carbohydrates; 0mg cholesterol.

22

Cooked Beans Mini Session

Pasta e Fagioli

Bean Casserole

Couscous-Bean Paella

Veggie-Bean Chili

Black Beans and Rice

Mexican Noodle Bake

Minestrone Soup

Ingredients List

Dairy

    1 cup fat-free plain yogurt

    8 ounces reduced-fat Cheddar cheese

    Parmesan cheese, grated

Bread/Pasta

    4 cups dried elbow macaroni

    1 ½ cups couscous

    2 cups long-grain rice

Vegetables

    7 large onions

2 large green bell peppers

1 small red bell pepper

4 large stalks celery

6 large carrots

10 cloves garlic

1 lime

10 ounces potatoes

Small head cabbage

Canned/Boxed

    5 (15-ounce) cans white beans

    6 (15-ounce) cans red kidney beans

4 (15-ounce) cans black beans

1 (15-ounce) can pinto beans

1 (16-ounce) can vegetable broth

5 (16-ounce) cans Italian-style
stewed tomatoes

2 (16-ounce) cans diced tomatoes

1 (4-ounce) can tomato paste

1 (16-ounce) can tomato sauce

20 ounces vegetable broth

1 (10-ounce) can water-packed
artichoke hearts

32 ounces salsa (mild, medium,
or hot)

24 ounces tomato juice

1 package taco seasoning mix

Parsley

Salt

Pepper

Bay leaf

Marjoram

Parsley

Saffron

Mustard, dry

Chili powder

Red pepper flakes

Cumin, ground

Oregano

Olive oil

Molasses

Soy sauce

Seasonings and Staples

Flour, all-purpose

Rosemary

Basil

Cayenne, ground

Frozen

1 cup frozen peas

1 cup frozen cut green beans

20 ounces frozen corn kernels

Preparation Instructions

Vegetable Prep

7 cups onion: chop

2½ cups green bell pepper: chop

1 cup red bell pepper: chop

½ cup celery: chop

1 cup celery: slice

5 large carrots: slice thinly

10 cloves garlic: mince

10 ounces potatoes: dice and store in pan full of cold water in refrigerator until ready to use.

2 cups cabbage: shred

Cheese Prep

8 ounces reduced-fat Cheddar cheese: grate

Misc. Prep

2 cups dry elbow macaroni: cook according to package directions until just tender, drain and rinse in cold water, and store in large pan full of cold water in refrigerator until ready to use.

Pasta e Fagioli

SERVES 6

1 cup chopped onion

½ cup chopped green bell pepper

½ cup sliced celery

1 cup thinly sliced carrots

2 tablespoons olive oil

2 tablespoons flour

½ teaspoon rosemary

1 teaspoon basil

¼ teaspoon ground cayenne

4 tablespoons minced parsley

1 (16-ounce) can Italian-style stewed tomatoes

1 (4-ounce) can tomato paste

1 teaspoon salt

½ teaspoon pepper

3 cloves garlic, minced

1 cup dried elbow macaroni

2 cans white beans, drained

1 quart vegetable broth

Advanced Prep

Chop onion and green pepper. Slice celery and carrots. Mince garlic.

Preparation

Heat the oil in a large skillet over medium heat, and sauté the onion, green pepper, celery, and carrots until soft. Remove from the heat. Stir in the flour, rosemary, basil, cayenne, parsley, stewed tomatoes, tomato paste, salt, pepper, and garlic until well blended. Stir in the macaroni, white beans, and broth. Spoon into a freezer bag. Label it, and freeze.

To Serve

Thaw the soup in the refrigerator at least 24 hours before serving.

To serve, place mixture into a stockpot, and add 4 cups water. Heat until boiling, and cook until the macaroni is tender.

Per Serving: 397.3 calories; 6.5g fat; 20.6g protein; 67.8g carbohydrates; 1mg cholesterol.

Bean Casserole

SERVES 6

Note: You can bake the casserole before freezing and reheat it by baking in a 325-degree oven for 20 minutes, or until heated through.

2 tablespoons olive oil

1 cup chopped onions

1 cup chopped green pepper

2 cloves garlic, minced

2 (16-ounce) cans Italian-style stewed tomatoes, drained and chopped

4 tablespoons minced parsley

1 teaspoon salt

½ teaspoon pepper

1 bay leaf

½ teaspoon marjoram

2 cans kidney beans, rinsed and drained

Advanced Prep

Chop onion and green pepper. Mince garlic.

Preparation

Heat the oil in a large skillet over medium heat, and sauté the onion, pepper, and garlic until soft. Remove from the heat. Stir in the tomatoes, parsley, salt, pepper, bay leaf, and marjoram. Stir in the beans. Spoon into a freezer bag. Label it, and freeze.

To Serve

Thaw the beans in the refrigerator at least 24 hours before serving. Preheat the oven to 325 degrees.

To serve, place beans into a 2-quart baking dish, cover, and bake for 1 hour.

Per Serving: 151.0 calories; 5.0g fat; 6.0g protein; 22.7g carbohydrates; 0mg cholesterol.

Couscous-Bean Paella

SERVES 6

—◆◆◆◆—

2 teaspoons olive oil

1 cup chopped onions

1 cup coarsely chopped red bell pepper

2¼ cups vegetable broth

1 (15-ounce) can black beans,
   drained and rinsed

1 can artichoke hearts

1½ cups couscous

1 cup frozen peas

⅛ teaspoon saffron

For Serving Day

1 lime, cut into wedges

Advanced Prep
Chop onion and red bell pepper.

Preparation
Heat the oil in a large skillet over medium heat, and sauté the onion and red bell pepper until soft. Remove from the heat. Stir in the vegetable broth, black beans, artichoke hearts, couscous, peas, and saffron. Pour into a freezer bag. Label it, and freeze.

To Serve
Thaw the paella in the refrigerator at least 24 hours before serving. To serve, place in a large saucepan, and heat over medium heat until heated through. Serves with the lime wedges.

Per Serving: 413.3 calories; 4.2g fat; 18.6g protein; 77.4g carbohydrates; 1mg cholesterol.

Veggie-Bean Chili

SERVES 6

¼ cup molasses

2 teaspoons dry mustard

2 teaspoons soy sauce

2 cloves garlic, minced

2 medium carrots, sliced

2 cups chopped onions

1 tablespoon chili powder

1 teaspoon red pepper flakes

2 (15-ounce) cans red kidney beans, drained and rinsed

1 (16-ounce) can diced tomatoes

1 (15-ounce) can pinto beans, drained and rinsed

For Serving Day

1 cup fat-free plain yogurt

Advanced Prep

Mince cloves garlic. Slice carrots. Chop onions.

Preparation

Stir together the molasses, mustard, and soy sauce in a bowl. Pour ½ cup water into a large skillet, and over medium heat, cook, covered, the onions, carrots, garlic, chili powder, and red pepper flakes until the carrots are almost tender. Uncover and cook until any liquid evaporates. Remove from the heat. Stir in the molasses mixture, kidney beans, tomatoes, and pinto beans. Spoon into a freezer bag. Label it, and freeze.

To Serve

Thaw the chili in the refrigerator at least 24 hours before serving.

To serve, place in a large saucepan, and heat over medium heat until heated through. Serve with a dollop of yogurt.

Per Serving: 284.5 calories; 1.4g fat; 14.6g protein; 56.0g carbohydrates; 1mg cholesterol.

Black Beans and Rice

SERVES 6

2 (15-ounce) cans black beans, drained and rinsed

32 ounces salsa (mild, medium, or hot)

3 cups tomato juice

20 ounces frozen corn kernels

2 cups uncooked long-grain rice

½ teaspoon ground cumin

½ teaspoon dried oregano

4 ounces (1 cup grated) reduced-fat Cheddar cheese

Advanced Prep

Rinse and drain beans. Grate cheese.

Preparation

Preheat the oven to 375 degrees.

Combine all the ingredients (except cheese) in a large bowl. Pour into a 9 × 13-inch baking dish, and bake for 1 hour. Remove from the oven. Cool. Wrap with foil. Put the cheese into a small freezer bag, and attach it to the baking dish. Label them, and freeze.

To Serve

Thaw the black-bean mixture in the refrigerator at least 24 hours before serving.

Preheat the oven to 350 degrees.

Sprinkle the mixture with the grated cheese. Bake for 15 to 20 minutes, or until the cheese is melted and beans and rice are heated through.

Per Serving: 471.3 calories; 3.0g fat; 25.7g protein; 90.4g carbohydrates; 4mg cholesterol.

Mexican Noodle Bake

6 SERVINGS

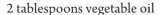

2 tablespoons vegetable oil

1 cup chopped onion

1 cup chopped green pepper

1 cup sliced celery

1 (16-ounce) tomato sauce

1 (16-ounce) can diced tomatoes

1 (15-ounce) can black beans,
   drained and rinsed

1 (15-ounce) can red kidney beans,
   undrained

1 package taco seasoning

2 cups dried elbow macaroni, cooked
   and cooled

4 ounces (1 cup grated) reduced-fat
   Cheddar cheese

Advanced Prep

Chop onion and green pepper. Slice celery. Cook macaroni according to package directions. Drain and rinse in cold water. Grate cheese.

Preparation

Heat the oil in a large skillet over medium heat, and sauté the onion, green pepper, and celery until soft. Stir in the tomato sauce, diced tomatoes, black beans, kidney beans, and taco seasoning, and cook for 10 minutes. Remove from the heat, and stir in the macaroni. Spread the mixture into a 9 × 13-inch baking dish. Wrap with foil. Place the grated cheese in a small freezer bag, and attach it to the baking dish. Label it, and freeze.

To Serve

Thaw the noodle dish in the refrigerator at least 24 hours before serving.

Preheat the oven to 375 degrees.

To serve, sprinkle the grated cheese over top, and bake, uncovered, for 45 minutes, or until the center is hot and the edges are bubbly.

Per Serving: 386.0 calories; 2.8g fat; 21.0g protein; 71.1g carbohydrates; 4mg cholesterol.

Minestrone Soup

SERVES 6

———————◆◀◆▶◆———————

2 teaspoons olive oil

1 cup chopped onions

1 cup thinly sliced carrots

3 cloves garlic, minced

2 (16-ounce) cans Italian-style stewed
  tomatoes, cut up and undrained

2 cups shredded cabbage, shredded

10 ounces potatoes, peeled and diced

2 (16-ounce) cans white beans

1 cup frozen cut green beans

1 cup dried elbow macaroni, cooked
  and cooled

1 tablespoon basil

½ teaspoon salt

¼ teaspoon pepper

For Serving Day

Grated Parmesan cheese, to taste

Advanced Prep

Chop onions. Mince garlic. Slice carrot. Pare and dice potatoes. Shred cabbage.

Preparation

Heat the oil in a large saucepan or Dutch oven over medium-high heat, and sauté the onion, carrots, and garlic until soft. Add the tomatoes, cabbage, and potatoes, and bring to a boil. Remove from the heat. Stir in the white beans, green beans, macaroni, basil, salt, and pepper. Stir to combine. Cool. Spoon into a freezer bag. Label it, and freeze.

To Serve

Thaw the soup in the refrigerator at least 24 hours before serving.

To serve, pour the soup and 5 cups water into a stockpot, and heat over medium heat until heated through. Sprinkle with the Parmesan cheese, and serve.

Per Serving: 390.3 calories; 3.7g fat; 21.9g protein; 71.1g carbohydrates;3mg cholesterol.

23
★ ★ ★

VEGETARIAN
MINI SESSION #1

Spinach Pizza
Mixed Veggie Soup

Cajun Stuffed Peppers
Cool Lime Burritos

Ingredients List

Dairy

1 large egg

1 (15-ounce) container reduced-fat
ricotta or cottage cheese

8 ounces reduced-fat mozzarella
cheese

Parmesan cheese, grated

8 ounces reduced-fat Cheddar cheese

Bread/Pasta

8 flour tortillas

Vegetables

2 large onions

1 bunch green onions

3 cloves garlic

3 large celery stalks

3 large carrots

1 bunch fresh parsley

6 small green, red, or yellow bell
peppers

1 lime

1 medium cucumber

Canned/Boxed

1 (8-ounce) jar pizza sauce

2 (16-ounce) cans Italian-style
stewed tomatoes

6 packets instant vegetable soup
seasoning mix

1 package Cajun-style rice and beans
mix

1 (4-ounce) can green chiles

1 (15-ounce) can red kidney beans

1 (15-ounce) can Mexican-style
stewed tomatoes

Seasonings and Staples

2 bay leaves

Cumin, ground

Cilantro

Pepper

Olive oil

Lime juice

White vinegar

Honey

Dijon mustard

Frozen

1 (16-ounce) package frozen bread
dough

2 (10-ounce) packages frozen
chopped spinach

1 small package frozen baby lima
beans

2 (10-ounce) packages frozen corn
kernels

Preparation Instructions

Vegetable Prep

2 cups onion: chop

½ cup green onion: slice

1½ cups celery: slice

1½ cups carrots: slice

3 cloves garlic: chop

6 small bell peppers (red, green, or yellow): cut in half lengthwise; remove seeds
and membranes.

1 medium cucumber: peel, seed, and drain

Cheese Prep

8 ounces reduced-fat mozzarella cheese: grate

4 ounces reduced-fat Cheddar cheese: grate

Misc. Prep

Frozen bread dough: thaw and let frozen dough rise according to package directions; punch down. Cover and let rest 5 minutes before using for pizza.

2 (10-ounce) packages frozen spinach: cook according to package directions, drain well, and pat dry.

Spinach Pizza

SERVES 6

◆◆◆◆◆◆

1 (16-ounce) package frozen bread
    dough, thawed

½ cup chopped onion

1 clove garlic, minced

1 tablespoon olive oil

2 (10-ounce) packages frozen
    chopped spinach

1 (15-ounce) container reduced-fat
    ricotta

1 egg, beaten

½ cup grated Parmesan cheese

1 (8-ounce) jar pizza sauce

8 ounces (2 cups) grated reduced-fat
    mozzarella cheese

Advanced Prep

Let frozen bread dough rise according to package directions; punch down. Cover, and let rest 5 minutes before using for pizza. Chop onion. Grate mozzarella cheese. Cook spinach according to package directions, drain well, and pat dry.

Preparation

Preheat the oven to 425 degrees. Line a 9 × 13-inch baking dish with heavy foil. Spray the foil thoroughly with nonstick cooking spray.

Using a rolling pin, roll the dough out to a 14 × 10-inch rectangle. Place it into the baking dish, patting it onto the bottom and up the sides. Prick the dough all over with the tines of a fork. Bake for 10 minutes, or until the dough starts to brown. Remove from the oven and let cool.

Heat the oil in a skillet over medium heat, and sauté the onion and garlic until soft. Remove from the heat. Mix together the spinach, ricotta, egg, Parmesan cheese, and onion mixture. Spread over the dough. Pour the pizza sauce over all. Freeze for 2 hours, or until firm. Lift the pizza and foil out of the pan. Wrap with foil. Put the grated mozzarella cheese in a small freezer bag, and attach it to the pizza. Label it, and freeze.

To Serve

To serve, preheat the oven to 375 degrees. Place the frozen pizza on a baking sheet, and remove the top foil. Bake for 1 hour, or until heated through. Top with cheese. Bake about 10 minutes more, or until cheese melts. Let stand 5 minutes, remove foil, and slice. Alternatively, thaw the pizza first for 24 hours in the refrigerator. Preheat the oven, and bake it for 20 minutes. Top with cheese, and bake 10 minutes more. Let stand for 5 minutes before slicing.

Per Serving: 514.5 calories; 23.3g fat 32.7g protein; 46.3g carbohydrates; 73mg cholesterol.

Mixed Veggie Soup

SERVES 6

◆◈◆

1½ cups diced onions

1½ cups sliced celery

1½ cups sliced carrots

2 (16-ounce) cans Italian-style
stewed tomatoes, cut up and
undrained

½ teaspoon pepper

2 cups frozen kernel corn

1 cup frozen baby lima beans

6 packets instant vegetable soup
seasoning mix

2 bay leaves

3 tablespoon chopped fresh parsley

Advanced Prep

Chop onions. Slice celery and carrots.

Preparation

Heat 1 cup water in a large saucepan or Dutch oven over medium heat, and cook the onion, celery, and carrots until soft. Stir in the tomatoes, corn, lima beans, seasoning mix, bay leaves, parsley, and pepper. Spoon into freezer bags. Label, and freeze.

To Serve

Thaw the soup in the refrigerator at least 24 hours before serving. To serve, pour the soup and 8 cups water into a stockpot, and heat over medium-high heat until heated through.

Per Serving: 343.5 calories; 5.7g fat; 13.1g protein; 64.6g carbohydrates; 3mg cholesterol.

Cajun Stuffed Peppers

SERVES 6

————◆◆◆————

1 (15-ounce) can Mexican-style diced tomatoes, undrained

1 package Cajun-style rice and beans mix

6 small green, red, or yellow bell peppers, or a combination of peppers

1 cup grated reduced-fat Cheddar cheese

Advanced Prep

Cut peppers in half lengthwise; remove seeds and membranes.

Preparation

Mix together the tomatoes, 1½ cups water, and the rice and beans mix in a large saucepan over heat. Bring to a boil, reduce the heat to low, cover, and cook for 10 minutes, or until the rice is tender.

Arrange each pepper half in a 9 × 13-inch baking dish. Divide rice and beans mixture between pepper halves, about ⅓ cup per pepper. Cover the pan with foil. Place grated cheese into small freezer bag, and attach to pan of stuffed peppers. Label it, and freeze.

To Serve

Thaw the peppers in the refrigerator at least 24 hours before serving. Preheat the oven to 350 degrees.

To serve, bake, covered, for 30 to 40 minutes, or until the peppers are tender. Uncover, and sprinkle with grated cheese. Bake 2 to 3 minutes more, or until cheese is melted.

Per Serving: 356.4 calories; 2.3g fat; 24.2g protein; 61.7g carbohydrates; 4mg cholesterol.

Cool Lime Burritos

SERVES 8

⬥◆⬥

⅓ cup lime juice

2 tablespoon white vinegar

2 tablespoons minced green chiles

1 tablespoon honey

2 teaspoons Dijon mustard

1 teaspoon grated lime zest

1 teaspoon ground cumin

2 cloves garlic, minced

1 (15-ounce) can red kidney beans,
   drained and rinsed

1 (10-ounce) package frozen corn
   kernels

½ cup sliced green onions

1 medium cucumber, peeled, seeded,
   and diced

2 tablespoons minced cilantro

For Serving Day

8 flour tortillas

Advanced Prep

Drain and rinse kidney beans.

Preparation

Stir together the lime juice, vinegar, chiles, honey, mustard, lime zest, cumin, and garlic in a nonreactive bowl. Pour the mixture into a large freezer bag. Add the beans, corn, onions, cucumber, and cilantro. Seal the bag, and rotate to mix the vegetables. Put the vegetable mixture bag and the tortilla bag into a larger bag. Label it, and freeze.

To Serve

Thaw the burrito mixture in the refrigerator at least 24 hours before serving.

To serve, stir to recombine. Drain the marinade off the vegetable mixture, and discard it. Warm tortillas, divide the bean mixture among the tortillas, and roll up to enclose.

Per Serving: 250.9 calories; 3.3g fat; 10.3g protein; 47.7g carbohydrates; 0mg cholesterol.

24

VEGETARIAN MINI SESSION #2

Vegetable Fried Rice
Ricotta-Broccoli Pie

Cheese-and-Veggie Quesadillas
Three-Cheese Lasagna

Ingredients List

Dairy

- 4 cups skim milk
- 7 large eggs
- 2 ounces Gruyère cheese
- 2 ounces reduced-fat mozzarella cheese
- 4 ounces reduced-fat Monterey Jack cheese
- 1 cup reduced-fat ricotta cheese
- Small container fat-free sour cream
- Parmesan cheese, grated
- Margarine

Bread/Pasta

- 1 pound spinach lasagna
- 12 flour tortillas
- Long-grain rice

Vegetables

- 1 large red bell pepper
- 1 bunch green onions
- 1 large leek
- 1 pound carrots
- 1 orange (for zest)
- 9 cloves garlic
- 1 small bunch fresh cilantro
- 1 piece fresh ginger

Canned/Boxed

    6 ounces canned black beans

    4 ounces canned green chiles

    1 cup salsa (mild, medium, or hot)

Seasonings and Staples

    Basil

    Nutmeg, ground

    Salt

    Pepper

    Sugar

Flour, all-purpose

Lime juice

Cider vinegar

Olive oil

Soy sauce

Oriental sesame oil

½ cup unsalted peanuts

Frozen

    2 (10-ounce) packages frozen
        broccoli pieces

Preparation Instructions

Vegetable Prep

    1 bunch green onions: slice

    1 bunch fresh cilantro: mince

    1½ cups leeks: wash and cut into strips

    1½ cups carrots: slice

    1½ cups red bell pepper: dice

    3 tablespoons fresh ginger root: grate

    9 cloves garlic: mince

    ½ cup unsalted peanuts: chop coarsely

    ½ teaspoon orange zest: finely grate orange part of orange rind

Cheese Prep

    4 ounces reduced-fat Monterey Jack cheese: grate

    2 ounces Gruyère cheese: grate

    2 ounces mozzarella cheese: grate

Misc. Prep

    10 ounces long-grain rice: prepare according to package directions

    2 (10-ounce) packages frozen broccoli: thaw, drain, and chop

    1 pound spinach lasagna noodles: prepare according to package directions, and
        rinse gently in cold water.

Vegetable Fried Rice

SERVES 6

4 eggs, beaten

½ cup sliced green onions, divided

½ cup minced fresh cilantro, divided

2 tablespoons soy sauce, divided

½ teaspoon sugar

1 tablespoon oriental sesame oil

1½ cups thinly sliced leeks

1½ cups thinly sliced carrots

1½ cups diced red bell pepper

3 tablespoons grated fresh ginger

6 cloves garlic, minced

1½ cups long-grain rice, cooked and cooled

½ cup coarsely chopped unsalted peanuts

3 tablespoons cider vinegar

½ teaspoon salt

Advanced Prep

Cook rice according to package directions. Slice green onion, leeks, and carrots. Chop bell pepper. Grate fresh ginger. Mince garlic. Chop peanuts.

Preparation

In a bowl, combine the eggs, ¼ cup green onions, ¼ cup cilantro, 2 tablespoons water, 1 tablespoon soy sauce, and the sugar. Spray a large skillet with nonstick cooking spray, and heat over medium-high heat. Cook the egg mixture until firm, and set aside. In another large skillet, heat the oil over medium-high heat, and sauté the leeks, carrots, and bell pepper until softened. Remove from heat. Stir in the ginger and garlic, and mix well. Add rice, peanuts, vinegar, salt, egg mixture, and the remaining green onions, cilantro, and soy sauce. Spoon into a large freezer bag. Label it, and freeze.

To Serve

Thaw the rice in the refrigerator at least 24 hours before serving.

To serve, heat the rice in a large skillet over medium-high heat until heated through. Add a sprinkling of sesame oil during cooking if the mixture seems dry.

Per Serving: 333.5 calories; 12.1g fat; 12.1g protein; 46.7g carbohydrates; 144mg cholesterol.

Ricotta-Broccoli Pie

SERVES 6

1 cup reduced-fat ricotta

1 cup skim milk

3 eggs

¼ cup grated Parmesan cheese

½ teaspoon orange zest

2 teaspoons olive oil

3 cloves garlic, minced

1 (10-ounce) package frozen broccoli, thawed, drained, and chopped

1 tablespoon basil

Advanced Prep

Zest orange peel. Mince garlic.

Preparation

Combine the ricotta, milk, and eggs in a blender or food processor, and blend until smooth. Add the Parmesan and orange zest, and process until combined. Heat the oil in a large skillet over medium heat, and sauté the garlic for a few seconds. Add the broccoli and basil, and cook 2 minutes. Combine the ricotta mixture and broccoli in a large bowl. Spoon into a freezer bag. Label it, and freeze.

To Serve

Thaw the broccoli mixture in the refrigerator at least 24 hours before serving.

Preheat the oven to 350 degrees.

To serve, squeeze the bag gently to recombine. Spray a 9-inch pie plate with non-stick cooking spray. Pour the mixture into the pie plate. Bake for 40 minutes, or until lightly browned and set. Let stand for 10 minutes before slicing.

Per Serving: 126.3 calories; 5.3g fat; 13.4g protein; 7.3g carbohydrates; 118mg cholesterol.

Cheese-and-Veggie Quesadillas

SERVES 6

◆▪◆▪◆

1 (6-ounce) can black beans, drained and rinsed

1 tablespoon lime juice

¼ cup chopped green chiles

¼ cup chopped fresh cilantro

¼ cup sliced green onions

1 cup fresh or frozen broccoli pieces

4 ounces (1 cup grated) reduced-fat Monterey Jack cheese

12 flour tortillas

For Serving Day

1 cup salsa (mild, medium, or hot)

3 tablespoons fat-free sour cream

Advanced Prep

Grate cheese. Drain and rinse canned black beans. Cook broccoli until just tender.

Preparation

In small bowl, mash beans and lime juice to form a paste. Stir in chiles, cilantro, and green onions. Place into labeled freezer bag. Place cooked broccoli into small freezer bag. Put the grated cheese into a small freezer bag. Store the beans, broccoli, cheese, and tortillas in a large freezer bag. Label it, and freeze.

To Serve

Thaw the bags in the refrigerator at least 24 hours before serving. Preheat the oven to 450 degrees.

To serve, spray 2 cookie sheets with nonstick cooking spray. Place 3 tortillas in a single layer onto each cookie sheet. Spread the bean mixture evenly among the tortillas, spreading it almost to the edge of each tortilla. Sprinkle on the broccoli pieces and the cheese. Top each tortilla with the remaining tortillas. Bake until the tortillas are lightly browned; halfway through baking time, switch cookie sheets in the oven. Slide the quesadillas onto a cutting board, and cut each into 6 wedges. Serve with cold salsa and sour cream.

Per Serving: 463.0 calories; 9.9g fat; 26.3g protein; 66.1g carbohydrates; 15mg cholesterol.

Three-Cheese Lasagna

SERVES 6

1 pound spinach lasagna, cooked and cooled

½ cup margarine

6 tablespoons flour

4 cups skim milk

2 ounces (½ cup grated) Gruyère cheese

2 ounces (½ cup grated) reduced-fat mozzarella cheese

¼ cup grated Parmesan cheese

¼ teaspoon salt

⅛ teaspoon pepper

Dash ground nutmeg

Advanced Prep

Prepare lasagna according to package directions. Rinse in cold water.

Preparation

Spray a deep casserole with generous amounts of nonstick cooking spray. Heat the margarine in a saucepan over low heat. Stir in the flour, and cook for 1 minute. Gradually stir in the milk, stirring constantly until the mixture in thick. Add the cheeses, salt, pepper, and nutmeg to sauce; stir until cheeses melt. Layer alternately the lasagne and the sauce in the casserole, ending with a layer of sauce. Wrap the casserole with foil. Label it, and freeze.

To Serve

Thaw the casserole in the refrigerator at least 24 hours before serving. Preheat the oven to 350 degrees.

To serve, uncover, and sprinkle the lasagna with extra Parmesan cheese. Bake for 45 minutes, until bubbling and golden brown.

Per Serving: 625.8 calories; 24.8g fat; 27.8g protein; 72.7g carbohydrates; 95mg cholesterol.

Vegetarian Mini Session #3

Dolmas
Baked Spaghetti

Vegetable Quiche
Spicy Chili Mac

Ingredients List

Dairy

⅔ cup fat-free plain yogurt

6 ounces reduced-fat Cheddar cheese

2 ounces reduced-fat Swiss cheese

5 eggs

Parmesan cheese

Bread/Pasta

Long-grain rice

12 ounces dried spaghetti

8 ounces dried elbow macaroni

Vegetables

2½ cups chopped onion

1 large cabbage head

4 large carrots

1 bunch green onions

1 lemon

1 small cucumber

Canned/Boxed

3 (14-ounce) cans diced tomatoes

1½ cups fat-free evaporated milk

3½ cups vegetable broth

1 (15-ounce) can Mexican-style stewed tomatoes

1 (15-ounce) can pinto beans

1 (15-ounce) can kidney beans

Seasonings and Staples	Salt
Basil	Pepper
Mint	Flour
Parsley	Olive oil
Italian seasoning	Pine nuts
Garlic powder	Dry currants
Chili powder	Soy sauce
Red pepper flakes	

Preparation Instructions

Vegetable Prep

1 bunch green onions: slice

2 large carrots: chop

2 large carrots: shred

3 medium onions: chop

12 large cabbage leaves: trim away tough stems, put leaves into boiling water briefly (about 30 seconds), remove from water using slotted spoon, and drain thoroughly.

Cheese Prep

6 ounces reduced-fat Cheddar cheese: grate.

2 ounces reduced-fat Swiss cheese: grate.

Misc. Prep

Rice: prepare according to package directions to make 1 cup, or use leftover rice.

12 ounces dried spaghetti: prepare according to package directions, drain and rinse in cold water, and store in large pan full of cold water in refrigerator until ready to use.

Dolmas

6 SERVINGS

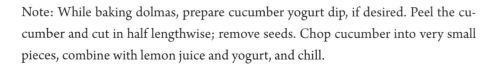

Note: While baking dolmas, prepare cucumber yogurt dip, if desired. Peel the cucumber and cut in half lengthwise; remove seeds. Chop cucumber into very small pieces, combine with lemon juice and yogurt, and chill.

12 large cabbage leaves, trimmed
  and washed

1 cup long-grain rice

8 green onions, chopped

½ cup pine nuts

½ cup currants

3 tablespoons olive oil

1½ teaspoons basil

1½ teaspoons mint

1½ teaspoons parsley

½ teaspoon salt

¼ teaspoon pepper

For Dip

  Juice of 1 lemon

  ⅔ cup fat-free plain yogurt

  ¼ cup peeled, seeded, and chopped
    cucumber

Advanced Prep

Trim away any tough stems from the cabbage leaves. Chop green onions.

Preparation

Preheat the oven to 375 degrees.

Blanch the leaves in boiling water for about 30 seconds. Using a slotted spoon, remove from the water and drain thoroughly. Lay the softened leaves flat on a clean surface. Stir together the rice, green onions, pine nuts, currants, oil, basil, mint, parsley, salt, and pepper, mixing well. Place 2 tablespoons of the rice filling onto each cabbage leaf, pressing it into a sausage shape. Fold the sides of the leaves over the filling and then roll up, jelly-roll fashion, to completely enclose the filling. Place the cabbage rolls seam-side down in a 9 × 13-inch baking dish. Pour hot water into baking dish to partially cover the rolls. Cover the baking dish with foil, pressing gently onto rolls.

Bake for 30 minutes. Remove from the oven. Cool. Wrap the dish in foil. Label it, and freeze.

To Serve

Thaw the dolmas in the refrigerator at least 24 hours before serving. Preheat the oven to 375 degrees.

To serve, bake for 15 minutes, or until heated through. Drain the cooking liquid from the dolmas, and arrange the dolmas on a serving plate. Combine the lemon juice, yogurt, and cucumber to make a sauce. Serve to spoon over the dolmas, if desired.

Per Serving: 392.7 calories; 14.6g fat; 13.3g protein; 61.5g carbohydrates; 0mg cholesterol.

Baked Spaghetti

SERVES 6

12 ounces dried spaghetti, cooked
  until just tender and drained

3 (14-ounce) cans diced tomatoes

1½ cups chopped onions

2 teaspoons Italian seasoning

4 ounces (1 cup grated) reduced-fat
  Cheddar cheese

3 tablespoons grated Parmesan cheese

Advanced Prep

Cook spaghetti noodles according to package directions, until just cooked. Chop onions. Grate cheese.

Preparation

Spray a 9 × 13-inch baking dish with nonstick cooking spray. Place the spaghetti in the baking dish, and pour the tomatoes over top. Sprinkle on the onions and Italian seasoning. Sprinkle on the Cheddar cheese, and then the Parmesan cheese. Wrap with foil. Label it, and freeze.

To Serve

Thaw the spaghetti in the refrigerator at least 24 hours before serving. Preheat the oven to 350 degrees.

To serve, bake for 30 to 35 minutes, or until hot and bubbly.

Per Serving: 289.6 calories; 3.4g fat; 14.1g protein; 50.7g carbohydrates; 6mg cholesterol.

Vegetable Quiche

SERVES 6

◆◂◆◂◆

Crust

- 1 cup cooked rice, white or brown
- 1 egg, beaten
- 1 teaspoon soy sauce

Filling

- 2 ounces (½ cup) reduced-fat cheddar cheese, grated
- 2 ounces (½ cup) reduced-fat Swiss cheese, grated
- ½ cup shredded carrot, shredded
- ¼ cup sliced green onions
- 1 tablespoon flour
- 4 eggs, beaten, or equivalent egg substitute
- 1½ cups fat-free evaporated milk
- ¼ teaspoon salt
- ¼ teaspoon pepper
- ¼ teaspoon garlic powder

Advanced Prep

Cook rice (or use leftover rice for crust). Grate cheeses. Shred carrots. Slice green onions.

Preparation

Preheat the oven to 350 degrees. Spray a 9-inch pie plate with nonstick cooking spray.

To make the crust, mix together the rice, egg, and soy sauce. Spread evenly in the prepared pan. Bake for 10 minutes. Remove from the oven.

To make the filling, stir together the cheeses, carrot, green onion, and flour in a bowl. Sprinkle over the crust. Mix together the eggs, milk, salt, pepper, and garlic powder, and pour over the cheese–vegetable mixture. Bake for 45 minutes, or until a knife inserted near the center comes out clean. Remove from the oven, and let stand 10 minutes before slicing, if serving right away or freezing in slices. Cool completely. Wrap with foil. Label it, and freeze.

To Serve

Thaw the quiche in the refrigerator at least 24 hours before serving. Preheat the oven to 350 degrees.

To serve, bake for 15 minutes, or until heated through, or serve it cold.

Per Serving: 192.1 calories; 5.1g fat; 15.7g protein; 19.8g carbohydrates; 185mg cholesterol.

Spicy Chili Mac

SERVES 6

◆◆◆

2 large carrots, chopped

1 cup chopped onions

3½ cups vegetable broth

1 (15-ounce) can Mexican-style
stewed tomatoes, cut up and
undrained

1 (15-ounce) can pinto beans,
undrained

1 (15-ounce) can red kidney beans,
undrained

3 tablespoons chili powder

½ teaspoon salt

½ teaspoon red pepper flakes

8 ounces dried elbow macaroni

For Serving Day

Fat-free plain yogurt or fat-free sour
cream (optional)

Advanced Prep

Chop carrots and onion.

Preparation

Heat ¼ cup water in a large skillet over medium heat, and cook the carrots and onions until just soft. Remove from heat. Add broth, tomatoes, pinto beans with liquid, kidney beans with liquid, chili powder, salt, and red pepper flakes. Stir in the macaroni. Spoon the mixture into a large freezer bag. Label it, and freeze.

To Serve

Thaw the dish in the refrigerator at least 24 hours before serving.

To serve, heat the mixture in a large saucepan over medium-high heat until heated through. Serve with plain yogurt or sour cream spooned on top, if desired.

Per Serving: 336.8 calories; 3.9g fat; 13.5g protein; 63.2g carbohydrates; 1mg cholesterol.

26
★ ★ ★

Eggplant Mini Session

Classic Ratatouille
Eggplant Bake

Stuffed Eggplant
Eggplant Penne

Ingredients List

Dairy
  Parmesan cheese, grated
  1½ cups fat-free plain yogurt
  4 ounces reduced-fat Cheddar cheese
  Margarine

Bread/Pasta
  10 ounces dried penne pasta
  Long-grain rice

Vegetables
  4 medium eggplants
  3 small eggplants
  6 medium zucchini

  1 green bell pepper
  1 red bell pepper
  6 large onions
  8 cloves garlic
  12 large tomatoes

Canned/Boxed
  2 (16-ounce) cans crushed tomatoes
  2 (16-ounces) cans stewed tomatoes
  1 (4-ounce) can green chiles

Seasonings and Staples
  Rosemary
  Salt

Pepper	Marjoram
Sugar	Cinnamon, ground
Red pepper flakes	Olive oil
Basil	Vegetable oil
Parsley	Red wine vinegar
Chili powder	Malt vinegar
Turmeric, ground	

Preparation Instructions

Cheese Prep

4 ounces reduced-fat Cheddar cheese: grate

Vegetable Prep

3 small eggplants: wrap in foil and bake 20 minutes at 350 degrees to soften.
Remove from oven; allow to cool. Cut eggplants in half; carefully scoop out
pulp, leaving a 1-inch-thick shell. Reserve scooped-out pulp.

2 medium-sized eggplants: cut into 1-inch cubes

2 medium-sized eggplants: cut into ¼-inch-thick slices

2 large onions: chop

4 large onions: peel and slice into rings

7 cloves garlic: mince

6 medium zucchini: halve lengthwise and slice thickly

1 green bell pepper: seed and cut into chunks

1 red bell pepper: seed and cut into chunks

4 large tomatoes: cut into chunks

Misc. Prep

Long-grain rice: prepare 1 cup cooked rice

Classic Ratatouille

SERVES 8

⬥◆⬥

⅓ cup olive oil

2 large onions, sliced

2 cloves garlic, minced

6 medium zucchini, halved lengthwise and thickly sliced

1 medium-sized eggplant, cut into
½-inch cubes

1 green pepper, seeded and cut into
chunks

1 red pepper, seeded and cut into
chunks

½ cup chopped parsley

1 teaspoon salt

1 teaspoon basil

4 large tomatoes, cut into chunks

Advanced Prep

Slice onions. Mince garlic. Cube eggplant. Slice zucchini. Seed and cut green and
red peppers into chunks. Cut tomatoes into chunks.

Preparation

Heat the oil in a large skillet over high heat, and sauté the onions and garlic until soft.
Add zucchini, eggplant, peppers, parsley, salt, and basil. Cover the skillet, reduce
the heat to medium-low, and cook for 30 minutes. If the mixture becomes dry, add
¼ cup of water. If mixture becomes too soupy and wet, remove the cover. Add the
tomato, and cook for 10 minutes more. Remove from the heat. Cool. Spoon into
large freezer bags. Label them, and freeze.

To Serve

Thaw the bags in the refrigerator at least 24 hours before serving.

To serve, heat over medium heat until heated through. Serve it hot or cold.

Per Serving: 148.3 calories; 9.5g fat; 3.2g protein; 15.6g carbohydrates; 0mg
cholesterol.

Eggplant Bake

SERVES 6

2½ tablespoons vegetable oil

2 large onions, peeled and sliced into rings

2 medium-sized eggplants, cut into ¼-inch-thick slices

8 tomatoes, sliced

2½ teaspoons salt, divided

⅔ cup malt vinegar

1 (4-ounce) can green chiles

1 (16-ounce) can stewed tomatoes, cut up and drained

¾ teaspoon chili powder

1 clove garlic, minced

¾ teaspoons ground turmeric

1 ½ cups fat-free plain yogurt

1 ¼ teaspoons ground black pepper

4 ounces (1 cup grated) reduced-fat Cheddar cheese

Advanced Prep

Slice eggplant into ¼-inch-thick slices. Slice onions into rings. Slice tomatoes. Grate cheese. Arrange the slices in a shallow baking dish and sprinkle with 1½ teaspoons of the salt. Pour the malt vinegar over the top, cover and marinate 30 minutes. Drain eggplant well; discard marinade liquid.

Preparation

Preheat the oven to 350 degrees. Spray a shallow ovenproof baking dish with non-stick cooking spray.

In large skillet, heat the vegetable oil and gently sauté onion rings until golden brown. Add chiles, remaining salt, tomatoes, chili powder, garlic, and turmeric. Mix well; simmer for 5 minutes. Remove sauce from heat and cool slightly. In blender or food processor, blend until smooth. Arrange half the eggplant slices in the prepared dish. Spoon half the tomato sauce over eggplant slices; cover with remaining eggplant; top with remaining tomato sauce and sliced tomatoes. In small bowl, combine yogurt, black pepper, and Cheddar cheese. Pour over tomato slices. Bake for 20 minutes. Remove from the oven. Cool. Wrap with foil. Label it, and freeze.

To Serve

Thaw the eggplant in the refrigerator at least 24 hours before serving. Preheat the oven to 375 degrees.

To serve, bake for 15 minutes, or until heated through and the topping is golden brown. Serve hot straight from the oven.

Per Serving: 242.0 calories; 9.5g fat; 10.9g protein; 33.7g carbohydrates; 10mg cholesterol.

Stuffed Eggplant

SERVES 6

———————◆◈◆———————

3 small eggplants

3 tablespoons margarine

1 large onion, finely chopped

2 cloves garlic, minced

1 (16-ounce) can stewed tomatoes, drained and cut up

1 cup long-grain rice, cooked

3 teaspoons chopped fresh marjoram

Pinch ground cinnamon

½ teaspoon salt

¼ teaspoon pepper

Advanced Prep

Preheat the oven to 350 degrees. Wrap eggplants in aluminum foil and bake 20 minutes to soften. Remove from oven; allow to cool. Cut the eggplants in half; carefully scoop out pulp, leaving a 1-inch-thick shell. Reserve the pulp. Chop onions. Cook rice.

Preparation

Heat the margarine in a large skillet over medium heat, and sauté the onion and garlic until soft. Chop the eggplant pulp coarsely, and stir it into the skillet. Cover and cook for 5 minutes. Stir the tomatoes, rice, marjoram, cinnamon, salt, and pepper into the eggplant mixture. Carefully pile the mixture into the eggplant shells. Wrap each stuffed eggplant half with foil. Place individually wrapped eggplants into a large freezer bag. Label it, seal and freeze.

To Serve

Thaw the eggplants in the foil wrappings in the refrigerator at least 24 hours before serving. Preheat the oven to 350 degrees.

To serve, remove the eggplant halves from the freezer bag, and keep them wrapped in foil. Place them onto a cookie sheet, and bake for 20 minutes.

Per Serving: 241.6 calories; 6.4g fat; 5.4g protein; 44.1g carbohydrates; 0mg cholesterol.

Eggplant Penne

SERVES 6

---

2 teaspoons olive oil

1 cup chopped onion

3 cloves garlic, minced

1 medium-sized eggplant, diced

2 cups canned crushed tomatoes

2 teaspoons red wine vinegar

½ teaspoon rosemary

½ teaspoon salt

½ teaspoon sugar

¼ teaspoon red pepper flakes

For Serving Day

10 ounces dried penne pasta

¼ cup grated Parmesan cheese

Advanced Prep

Chop onion. Mince garlic. Dice eggplant.

Preparation

Heat the oil in a large skillet over medium heat, and sauté the onion and garlic until the onion is soft. Add the eggplant and ½ cup water, and bring to a boil. Reduce the heat to low, cover, and cook for 5 minutes. Remove from the heat. Stir in the tomatoes, vinegar, rosemary, salt, sugar, and red pepper flakes. Cool. Spoon into a freezer bag. Label it, and freeze.

To Serve

Thaw the eggplants in the foil wrappings in the refrigerator at least 24 hours before serving.

To serve, cook the penne according to package directions. Heat the eggplant–tomato mixture in a large skillet over medium-high heat, until heated through. Toss the penne and eggplant mixture together, and sprinkle with Parmesan cheese.

Per Serving: 254.3 calories; 6.4g fat; 9.4g protein; 46.9g carbohydrates; 3mg cholesterol.

APPENDIX A:
FREEZING TIMES CHART

Freezing for longer than the recommended times could mean less-than-perfect food after thawing. For best results, use the following guidelines:

Baked goods (breads, muffins, and rolls) = 2 to 3 months

Beef (ground), cooked = 2 to 3 months

Beef (ground), raw = 4 to 6 months

Beef (non-ground), cooked = 4 to 6 months

Beef (non-ground), raw = 7 to 9 months

Casseroles = 2 to 6 months

Chili = 4 to 6 months

Cookies = 4 to 6 months

Fish, cooked = 2 to 3 months

Fish, raw pieces = 12 months

Gravy = 1 to 2 months

Meatloaf, meatballs = 3 to 4 months

Meat pies = 2 months

Pancakes/waffles = 6 months

Pasta recipes = 2 to 3 months

Pizza = 2 months

Pizza dough = 6 months

Pork, cooked = 1 to 2 months

Potatoes, cooked = 1 to 2 months

Poultry, cooked = 2 to 3 months

Poultry, raw = 9 to 12 months

Quiche (cooked or uncooked) = 3 months

Rice, cooked = 3 to 4 months

Sauces = 4 to 6 months

Seafood, cooked = 2 months

Seafood, raw = 12 months

Soups, stews = 2 to 3 months

Vegetables, blanched = 10 to 12 months

APPENDIX B:
RECIPE EQUIVALENTS

Recipes will often call for 2 cups of diced onions or 3 cups of grated cheese. This can make it difficult to decipher how many whole onions to buy or how many pounds of cheese to add to your shopping list. The following list of equivalents is approximate.

Vegetables/Fruits

1 medium onion = 1 cup diced
1 medium green pepper = 1 cup diced
3 ounces fresh mushrooms = 1 cup sliced
1 pound carrots = 3 cups sliced or diced
2 large celery ribs = 1 cup sliced or diced
1 medium tomato = 1 cup chopped
1 medium clove garlic = 1 teaspoon minced
1 medium potato = 1 cup sliced or chopped
1 medium apple = 1 cup chopped
1 lemon = 3 tablespoons juice

Dairy

4 ounces (¼ pound) cheese = 1 cup grated or cubed

1 pound block of cheese = 4 cups grated or cubed

1 cup heavy whipping cream = 2 cups whipped

2 cups margarine or butter = 1 pound

Bread/Pasta/Rice/Beans

1½ slices bread = 1 cup fresh breadcrumbs

24 saltine crackers = 1 cup fine crumbs

8 ounces dried noodles = 4 to 5 cups cooked

12 ounces dried spaghetti = 4 cups cooked

1 cup uncooked long-grain rice = 3 cups cooked

Meats

1 pound ground beef or turkey = 2½ cups browned

3 to 4 pound whole chicken = 4 cups cooked meat

1 medium chicken breast = 1 cup cubed

1 pound ham = 3 cups cubed or ground

8 slices bacon = ½ cup crumbled

1 pound stew meat = 2 cups cubed

Misc.

¼ pound nuts = 1 cup chopped

APPENDIX C: RECOMMENDED RESOURCES

Freezer Meal Books

I've discovered that many people who enjoy cooking for the freezer also like to collect cookbooks on the topic. If you're looking for more information, there's a great deal available. If you order one of these books directly from the author, be sure to mention that you read about their resources in *Frozen Assets Lite and Easy*. As an author, I know it's always helpful and fun to discover how people first find out about your books.

Several of the listed resources are currently out of print. If you're interested in reading these books, check with your local library to see if they're available through an interlibrary loan. I found copies of these out-of-print resources at local yard sales and thrift stores.

Note: My two *Frozen Assets* books and the book *Once-a-Month Cooking* are the only freezer-cooking books I've found that provide prepared meal plans. The other books require the reader to develop their own meal plans from the included recipes.

★ *Frozen Assets: How to Cook for a Day and Eat for a Month,* by Deborah Taylor-Hough.

My original freezer-meal book. Inexpensive recipes, step-by-step instructions, money-saving ideas, family-friendly. Contains a complete Thirty-Day Meal Plan, a Two-Week Meal Plan, and a special Ten-Day Holiday Meal Plan. Available through bookstores and libraries.

★ *Bake and Freeze Chocolate Desserts,* by Elinor Klivans.

Wow! Chocolate cooking for the freezer. A hundred and twenty recipes for chocolate treats that can be made ahead frozen to be eaten weeks, or even months, later. Great idea during the holidays. Available through bookstores and libraries.

★ *Cooking Ahead,* by Mary Carney.

A home-schooling mother of four, minister's wife, frequent seminar speaker, and freelance writer, Mary Carney has depended on her *Cooking Ahead* techniques to simplify her busy life.

★ *Cooking for the Freezer,* by Myra Waldo.

An older book that is excellent for examples of the types of things that freeze well.

★ *Cook Now, Serve Later,* by Reader's Digest Books.

A full-range general cookbook of 425 recipes especially designed to be prepared in advance and stored in the refrigerator or freezer. Available in bookstores and libraries.

★ *Dinner's in the Freezer: More Mary & Less Martha,* by Jill Bond.

Contains general information on Christian homemaking, including some information on cooking for the freezer. Helpful charts. Available through bookstores and libraries.

★ *The Complete Do-Ahead Cookbook: Southern Living,* by Ann H. Harvey.

Large format, hardbound book. A large number of recipes for the freezer along with recipes that aren't frozen, but can be prepared hours (or days!) ahead of time to be served later. Available through bookstores and libraries.

★ *Don't Panic—Dinner's in the Freezer,* by Susie Martinez, Bonnie Garcia, and Vanda Howell.

This book was developed by a group of friends that cooked together and then began sharing what they were doing with others. The book is small, spiral-bound, lays flat, and it offers a nice collection of recipes.

★ *Farm Journal Freezing and Canning Cookbook: Prized Recipes from the Farms of America,* by the food editors of *Farm Journal.*

Country women have always been known for their well-stocked pantries. Tips, recipes, and helpful hints.

★ *Better Homes and Gardens Fix & Freeze Cookbook,* by Gerald Knox, ed.

Excellent recipes, tips, and full-color photographs.

★ *The Freezer Cooking Manual from 30 Day Gourmet: A Month of Meals Made Easy,* by Nanci Slagle and Tara Wohlenhaus.

This is the updated version of the *30 Day Gourmet* notebook. Emphasizes sharing your cooking day with a friend. Charts and planning sheets to simplify cooking with someone else. Features photos, humor, and it is spiral-bound.

★ *Guests Without Stress: A Cookbook: Great Recipes and Menus to Make Ahead* by Elizabeth Hill, Martha Star, and Ann Upton.

Recipes and menus to make ahead. Available in bookstores and libraries.

★ *Better Homes and Gardens Make-Ahead Cookbook,* by Don Dooley, ed.

Recipes to make now and serve later, but not all recipes are designed for freezer cooking.

★ *Month of Meals,* by Kelly Machel.

A small book with a three-ring binder format. Friendly recipes.

★ *Once a Month Cooking: A Proven System for Spending Less Time in the Kitchen and Enjoying Delicious, Homemade Meals Everyday,* by Mary Beth Lagerborg and Mimi Wilson.

This book revolutionized the way I feed my family. The recipes are a bit on the gourmet and expensive side. It offers several complete meal plans, including a low-fat two-week version.

★ *Once and For All Cooking,* by Stephanie Stephens.

A spiral-bound cookbook in a large format. The author is a trained gourmet cook, and the recipes are geared toward gourmet tastes (they may not be appealing to small children, but the recipes look tasty to me).

★ *Prevention's Low-Fat, Low-Cost Freezer Cookbook: Quick Dishes for and from the Freezer,* by Sharon Sanders.

More than 220 recipes. Published by Prevention Health Books.

Cooking–Related Books

★ *365 Quick, Easy and Inexpensive Dinner Menus,* by Penny E. Stone.

This book contains more simple-to-prepare and family-pleasing recipes than I've ever seen collected into a single volume.

★ *Cheapskate in the Kitchen,* by Mary Hunt.

Learn to prepare delicious gourmet meals for a fraction of the cost of restaurant dining. I contributed several recipes to this book.

★ *Desperation Dinners,* by Beverly Mills and Alicia Ross.

The answer to every desperate cook's prayers. Features delicious, healthy, and home-cooked meals that can be prepared in 20 minutes.

★ *Eat Healthy for $50 a Week: Feed Your Family Nutritious, Delicious Meals for Less,* by Rhonda Barfield.

Yes, it really is possible to feed your family healthy meals for $50 per week. Barfield shows you how (recipes included).

★ *Healthy Foods: An Irreverent Guide to Understanding Nutrition and Feeding Your Family Well,* by Leanne Ely.

This fun and practical cookbook takes you step-by-step through nutrition fundamentals and provides over 100 taste-tested recipes even the kids will love. Being healthy has never been easier!

★ *Mix-n-Match Recipes*, by Deborah Taylor-Hough.

Simple and creative recipes using common ingredients. A great way to use up leftovers. Soup, quiche, skillet meals, casseroles, dessert breads, and more. Available in bookstores and libraries.

★ *More-With-Less Cookbook*, by Doris Janzen Longacre.

The classic, thoughtful cookbook published by the Mennonites. Every kitchen needs this book.

★ *The New Laurel's Kitchen, A Handbook for Vegetarian Cookery and Nutrition*, by Laurel Robertson, Carol Flinders, and Brian Ruppenthal.

Vegetarian cooking at its best.

★ *Not Just Beans: Fifty Years of Frugal Family Favorites*, by Tawra Jean Kellam.

More than 500 recipes and 400-plus tips.

★ *Make-A-Mix Cookery*, by Karine Eliason, Nevada Harward, and Madeline Westover.

Make your own healthy homemade mixes. Save time and money, and you'll control the ingredients, so you'll know the mixes are healthy for your family. Many mixes make great gift ideas, too.

★ ★ ★

ABOUT THE AUTHOR

Deborah Taylor-Hough is a freelance writer who runs a household and home-schools three children, all while balancing a limited budget and maintaining many outside interests.